TRADE, COMMERCE AND SECURITY CHALLENGES
CHALLENGES
IN THE ASIA-PACIFIC REGION

TRADE, COMMERCE AND SECURITY CHALLENGES IN THE ASIA-PACIFIC REGION

Edited by

Maj Gen YK Gera (Retd)

BASED ON PROCEEDINGS OF
NATIONAL SECURITY SEMINAR 2012
HELD AT USI, NEW DELHI
ON 01-02 NOV 2012

(Established 1870)

United Service Institute of India
New Delhi

Vij Books India Pvt Ltd
New Delhi (India)

Published by

Vij Books India Pvt Ltd
(Publishers, Distributors & Importers)
2/19, Ansari Road
Delhi – 110 002
Phones: 91-11-43596460, 91-11-47340674
Fax: 91-11-47340674
e-mail: vijbooks@rediffmail.com

CONTENTS

CONCEPT NOTE

Trade, Commerce and Security Challenges in the Asia-Pacific Region

The Asia-Pacific-Region is a dynamic but complex area where much of the history of the 21st Century will be scripted. Although the strategic and economic importance of the Region continues to grow, challenges of reconciling national interests with regional and global interests continue. Security architectures during the Cold War were based primarily on military alliances. However, the need today is to base these architectures on shared values, interests and challenges. We need to not only define but believe in these universal values, regional and international interests and global challenges. We need to do a lot more here.

Rapid increase in international trade and financial flows coupled with fiercely competitive multi-national companies, supported by global supply chain networks, offer tremendous opportunities for trade and investment. The Region represents 55 per cent of global GDP and 44 per cent of world trade and is home to some of the largest economies as also to the world's largest militaries. Security plays a vital role in keeping the economy growing by keeping the transportation networks secure as also by protecting the economic and financial infrastructure from attack and undertaking action to ensure speedy recovery of commerce following an attack or natural disaster.

Despite greater economic integration and strategic dialogue, there persists mistrust and brinkmanship which could jeopardize peace, stability and economic growth in the Region. Hence there is a need to look at linkages between trade and commerce, energy, environment, maritime issues and their broader linkages to geopolitics, strategy and security.

Trade and Commerce in the Asia-Pacific Region and its Impact on Security (Session–1)

This session will primarily examine economic issues as they are the fundamental drivers of all other issues. We need to examine the linkages between trade and security. Do trade and economic linkages bring about greater stability or do they curtail the options of comparatively smaller economies?

While the evolution of Asia's Trade Architecture has had an impact on regional and global economy, there is a need to analyse how the Region reacted to economic challenges so as to draw lessons for the future. To understand the strength of the economic institutions, we need to analyse whether the responses were driven by these institutions or were led by powerful nations deciding amongst themselves in the background? Are any remedial measures required?

A priority for the governments in this region is to secure efficient trade, most of which is transported over the seas. What should be done to enhance the security of commercial shipping and sea borne trade as well as to promote regional security and economic development?

The world is looking upto the region to provide an impetus to the world economy. Will the Asia-Pacific be a growth leader? What will be the effect of an economic down turn in the Asia-Pacific-Region on the global stage? And last but not the least; will narrow, nationalistic trade and economic considerations be the drivers of strategic instability?

In the regional context, we have bi-lateral as well as multi-lateral socio-politico-economic arrangements, dialogues and partnerships. How can we co-opt multi-lateral agendas into the bi-lateral sphere? Can we construct a multi-lateral framework which can channel some of its positive aspects into the bi-lateral framework and vice-versa?

Energy, Environmental and Maritime Security (Session–2)

Energy security affects economic performance and political stability. While many sources of energy exist, oil continues to be at the heart of the region's energy challenges. What are the prospects for regional cooperation in the energy security domain? Suggest policy options which will contribute to energy security.

Alternate Energy – will it be a game changer? What will be its geopolitical impact? Also, how will it impact environmental considerations and economic and defence needs?

Some of the environmental issues that need to be discussed are:-

(a) Security implications of climate change including the aspects of food security.

(b) Trans-national rivers and sustainable management of water resources.

(c) Sustainable use of natural resources and the challenges of "green growth".

(d) Trans-boundary air pollution.

(e) Armed forces and environmental pollution.

Maritime security is an indispensable and fundamental condition for the welfare and economic security of the global community. The challenges arise not only from piracy, terrorism and environmental issues but also from conflicting national interests and the urge for politico-military dominance. Varying interpretations of freedom of navigation adds to the complexity of the security challenge. Protecting maritime freedom will require finding the right balance between the rights of nations and the freedom of the world community. All nations will have to abide by universally accepted laws and principles. Suggest ways and means to evolve an open, transparent and inclusive maritime security structure that will ensure the protection and preservation of maritime freedom. Also suggest measures to facilitate maritime security cooperation.

While traditional threats have enlarged to include non-traditional threats like climate change, pandemics, non-state actors, cyber and economic crimes etc; we continue to look at these primarily through the military-diplomatic lens. Is there a need today for greater inter-action between the politico-military-diplomatic players and scientists and experts from the non-traditional security fields? Will this necessitate new security architecture?

Future Security Challenges and Opportunities (Session–3)

Challenge of reconciling national interests with regional and global interests persists leading to mistrust and brinkmanship. What is the regional security outlook for the period 2013-2015?

Has the rise of emerging powers added to a sense of insecurity in others? How does this impact evolving fair and sustainable security architecture? What role will deterrence play in the evolving security architecture? Economic growth has underpinned military modernization and military capability growth in most of the countries in the Region. Will this lead to a balance of power and greater stability or will this lead to tensions and instability? The Indian Ocean and the Pacific Ocean are now being increasingly viewed as a single strategic system. What are the implications? What are the challenges in the Space and Cyber domain? Will the responses continue to be at the national level or can a regional / global response be worked out?

Are regional conflict prevention and conflict resolution capacities adequate? What can be done to make these more effective?

Can we have comprehensive security without cooperative security? Can confidence building measures by themselves be enough or do we need confidence and security building measures?

PARTICIPANTS

Lieutenant General PK Singh, PVSM, AVSM (Retd)

Lieutenant General PK Singh is the Director of the United Service Institution of India, New Delhi since 1st January 2009. During his military career spanning 41 years he participated in active counter-insurgency operations and the Indo-Pakistan War of 1971. He retired from active service in September 2008 as C-in-C (Army Commander). His academic qualifications include M Sc, M Phil and a Post Graduate Diploma in Business Management. He is a Council Member of the Indian Council of World Affairs, and Advisor to the Fair Observer, USA.

Ambassador Kanwal Sibal, IFS (Retd)

Kanwal Sibal is a career diplomat who has held several ambassadorial level positions. He was India's Ambassador to Turkey (1989-1992) and Deputy Chief of Mission in the United States (1992-1995), with the rank of Ambassador. He served thereafter as India's Ambassador to Egypt (1995-1998) and Ambassador to France (1998-2002). He also served as India's Ambassador to Russia (2004-2007). He retired from service in November 2003 as Foreign Secretary.

Ambassador Sibal writes regularly for national journals and periodicals on international affairs. He is an Editorial Consultant to *The Indian Defence Review* and Foreign Affairs Editor of *Force* - the two most prominent defense and security related publications.

Dr Daesung Song

Dr. Daesung Song, is President of the Sejong Institute of Republic of Korea since 01 January 2009. He has served in Korean Air Force and retired as a Brigadier General in 1996. He has done Ph.D. from University of Michigan USA. He has authored a number of books on security and strategic issues. In the year 2008, two of his books titled "North Korea Policy and Korean National Security" and "Transformation of Korea-US Alliance and Korean National Security" got published.

Major General YK Gera (Retd)

Maj Gen YK Gera (Retd) is a telecommunication Engineer. He has authored book titled "Non-Conventional Threat Perceptions in the Indian Context". He has edited the books "Peace and Stability in Afghanistan: The Way Ahead" and "Peace and Stability in Asia Pacific Region: Assessment of the Security Architecture". He is Consultant and Head (Research) with Centre for Strategic Studies and Simulation (CS3), United Service Institution of India.

Mr T. C. Venkat Subramanian

T. C. Venkat Subramanian is Chairman and Managing Director of Export-Import Bank of India (Exim Bank). Prior to this he was Managing Director and CEO of Exim Bank. He joined Exim Bank of India in 1982 when the Bank was set up. He actively participated in the setting up of Exim Bank as a model public sector organization with a professional work culture.

Mr. Venkat Subramanian brings to this position diverse experience in industrial and export financing. Mr. Venkat Subramanian is also Chairman of two Exim Bank joint ventures – Global Procurement Consultants Ltd., and Global Trade Finance Pvt. Ltd. He is also Director on the Boards of Agricultural Finance Corporation and Small Farmers' Agri-Business Consortium.

Ms Tsun-Tzu Hsu

Kristy Hsu is Associate Research Fellow and Section Chief at the Taiwan WTO Centre, and Programme Coordinator at the Taiwan ASEAN Studies Centre (TASC), Chung Hua Institution for Economic Research (CIER), Taiwan (R.O.C). Her areas of research include international trade policy and economic/trade law, trade and development issues, regional integration, and gender issues. Kristy obtained her LL.M from the School of Law, Soochow University, Taiwan.

She is Advisory Member to the Trade and Development Committee, ROC National Confederation of Industries, International Affairs Committee, ROC Chamber of Commerce, and adviser to the Chinese National Association of Industry and Commerce's, (CNAIC's) monthly publication CNAIC Magazine, and Standing Supervisor to Taiwan Women Film/Video Association.

Commodore Ranjit B. Rai (Retd)

Cmde Ranjit B. Rai (Retd) attended Yarrow Shipyard, HMS Dryad and RN Staff College UK and has Commanded three ships and India's Naval Academy. He has served as Director Operations (DNO) and Intelligence (DNI) at NHQ. Cmde Rai has served as a Defence Adviser in the Indian High Commission Singapore and South East Asia for 4 years with visits to Australia, USA and China.

Cmde Ranjit Rai Completed Ship Management Course at IIM Ahmedabad, and served as Indian Representative for USA's largest LASH Project carrier Waterman Steam Ship Corporation till 2003. Presently he is the Vice President of Indian Maritime Foundation. He is also a Defence Analyst and Broadcaster.

Vice Admiral PS Das, PVSM, AVSM, VSM (Retd)

Vice Admiral PS Das retired from the Indian Navy in 1998 as Commander-in-Chief of the Eastern Naval Command. After retirement, Admiral Das was nominated member of a Task Force constituted by the Government to review Higher Defence Management in India. He was elected to the Executive Councils of the Institute of Defence Studies and Analyses (IDSA) and the United Service Institution of India (USI), two of the leading Think Tanks in India dealing with security and strategic issues.

He is currently serving a fourth term in the Council of the IDSA. He is a graduate of the Naval War College, USA, and holds a Master's degree in Business Administration. Admiral Das is well known in the strategic community. He writes regularly for national newspapers and journals and has more than 250 published articles to his credit. He is a guest speaker at the National Defence College, at other War Colleges of the Indian Armed Forces, at the Foreign Service Institute and at several seminars and conferences abroad. He is a member of important strategic dialogues with the USA, China, Japan, Turkey and Singapore and has served as member of the National Security Advisory Board.

Dr Annika Bolten-Drutschmann

She Joined the German Foreign Service in 2008 after completing a PhD in International Political Economy at the London School of Economics and

Political Science. Previously she read Politics, Philosophy and Economics in the UK and in the USA and obtained a MSc in Politics of the World Economy at the London School of Economics and Political Science.

She Served as Interim Head of Culture and Press Affairs in Singapore (2009) and as Political Officer in Jakarta with responsibilities for ASEAN, Timor-Leste and Indonesia (2009-2012). Took up her post as Policy Planning Staff in Berlin in the summer of 2012 where she focuses on Asia-Pacific and Central Asia affairs.

Vice Adm Arun Kumar Singh, PVSM, AVSM, NM (Retd)

Vice Admiral Arun Kumar Singh served in the Navy for 40 years. During his service career he was a nuclear submariner who commanded various warships, submarines, submarine bases and submarine squadrons. As Director General of the Indian Coast Guard he signed the Hotline Agreement in 2005, with the Maritime Security Agency of Pakistan, and also exercised with the Coast Guards of Japan, South Korea and Maldives. He also commanded the Indian Coast Guard rescue and relief operations in India, Sri Lanka and Maldives, after the Tsunami disaster of 26 December 2004. He had tenure as Commander-in-Chief of the Joint Andaman & Nicobar Command. Later he took over as Flag Officer Commanding-in-Chief, Eastern Naval Command, from where he retired in 2007. He is a prolific writer and speaker on issues maritime, nuclear, international affairs, and is an internationally respected strategic analyst.

Senior Colonel Le Kim Dung

Senior Colonel Le Kim Dung is a serving officer. He is posted as Director of the Department of International Relations Studies, Institute for Defense Strategy, Ministry of National Defence of Vietnam. He is an Engineer in Military Technology. His area of interest is Strategic Issues and International Relations

Dr. Ivan Safranchuk

Dr. Ivan Safranchuk graduated in 1998 from the Moscow State Institute of International Relations (MGIMO). Dr. Safranchuk received the degree of candidate of sciences (Russian equivalent of Ph.D.) from Academy of Military Sciences for the thesis on post-Cold War nuclear strategy. From

1997 to 2001 he worked at the PIR Centre for Policy Studies. In 2001 he joined Washington-based think-tank Centre for Defense Information to open a branch office in Russia. In 2006 CDI was renamed into World Security Institute (WSI). In 2006 Dr. Safranchuk left WSI, but served advisor to WSI in the next two years. From 2003 Dr. Safranchuk lectures at MGIMO. From 2007 he publishes analytical magazine "Great Game: politics, business, security in Central Asia" and heads consulting firm LaTUK, specializing on energy, politics and security in Central Asia and neighbouring regions.

Through 2010 Dr. Safranchuk led the project, sponsored by Russian MFA, to research regional perspectives on the Afghani situation. In 2011 Dr. Safranchuk was appointed deputy director at the Institute of Contemporary International Studies (*Diplomatic* Academy, Russian MFA).

Major General Dato' Pahlawan Dr William R. Stevenson

Maj Gen Dato' Pahlawan Dr. William R. Stevenson is the Executive Director of Malaysian Institute of Defence and Security (MIDAS) which was established in April 2010 under the purview of Ministry of Defence, Malaysia. He plans and supervises MIDAS activities which aim to generate new ideas through forums, debates, seminars and publishing of journal on defence and security.

Professor Richard Rigby

Richard Rigby graduated with First Class Honor's in History from the ANU in 1970, and went on to do his PhD. Richard joined Australia's Department of Foreign Affairs in 1975, where he worked until the end of 2001. His postings included Tokyo, Beijing (twice), Shanghai, London and Israel (Ambassador, 2000-2001). He then joined the Office of National Assessments as Assistant Director-General, responsible for North and South Asia, where he worked until taking up his current position with the ANU China Institute in April 2008.

While engaged in government work, Professor Rigby continued to pursue his academic interests with a series of translations, book reviews and articles on China-related topics. His personal interests in Chinese studies are primarily literary and historical, but his profession has ensured a thorough immersion in all aspects of contemporary China and other major Asian cultures.

Dr Brendan Taylor

Dr Brendan Taylor is Head of the Strategic and Defence Studies Centre, Australian National University. He is a specialist on great power strategic relations in the Asia-Pacific, economic sanctions, and Asian security architecture. His publications have featured in leading academic journals: International Affairs, Survival, Asian Security, Review of International Studies and the Australian Journal of International Affairs. He is the author of Sanctions as Grand Strategy, which was published in the International Institute for Strategic Studies (IISS) Adelphi book series, as well as American Sanctions in the Asia Pacific (Routledge, 2010).

Professor Swaran Singh

Professor Singh teaches Diplomacy and Disarmament Studies at the Centre for International Politics, Organisation and Disarmament, School of International Studies, Jawaharlal Nehru University (New Delhi). He is President of Association of Asia Scholars, General Secretary of Indian Association of Asian and Pacific Studies and Member, Bangkok-based Asian Scholarship Foundation's Regional Review Committee for South Asia. Professor Singh is Visiting Professor, University of Peace (Costa Rica) and Lady Sri Ram College (New Delhi). He is a former Visiting Faculty of the Beijing University, Fudan University, Xiamen University and Shanghai Institute of International Studies.

Professor Singh has travelled and written extensively on Asian Affairs, China's foreign and security policy issues with special focus on China-India confidence building measures as also on Arms Control and Disarmament, Peace and Conflict Resolution, India's foreign and security policy issues.

Sr Col Do Mai Khanh

Mrs. Do Mai Khanh is Senior Colonel, Deputy of the Institute for Defence International Relations (IDIR), MoD of Vietnam. She assists the Director in all multilateral matters relating to defence and security activities that Ministry of National Defense of Vietnam participates, especially those within ASEAN and ARF framework.

Previously, Mrs Khanh was a course member of the Centre of Defence Strategic Study/ Australian Defence College from Jan 2011 to Dec 2011.

She has also served in various positions both in the Department for Foreign Relations (DFR) and the Institute for Defence International Relations (IDIR). She was an Assistant Defense Attaché of Vietnam to the US from May 2005 to March 2009.

Dr Satoru Nagao

Dr. Satoru Nagao is a Research Fellow at Ocean Policy Research Foundation, Japan. He did his PhD in 2011 from Gakushuin University. The theme for his PhD was– "The Development of India's War Strategy: How to use Military Power as Dominant Power in South Asia?" Dr. Satoru Nagao has written a number of articles on strategic and security issues.

Air Chief Marshal SP Tyagi, PVSM, AVSM, VM, ADC (Retd)

Air Chief Marshal S P Tyagi is a former Chief of the Air Staff. He was commissioned in the fighter stream of the IAF on 31 December 1963. He actively participated in the 1965 and 1971 wars. Prior to taking over as Chief of Air Staff, he was commanding Western Air Command in the rank of Air Marshal.He is one of the few officers to have the distinction of commanding three Air Commands, Central, South Western and Western Air Command.

Dr Eiichi Katahara

Eiichi Katahara is Director, Regional Studies Department at the National Institute for Defense Studies, Japan Ministry of Defense. He is Editor-in-Chief, East Asian Strategic Review 2012 (Tokyo, NIDS, 2012). Prior to joining the NIDS, he was Professor of International Relations at Kobe Gakuin University; a visiting fellow at Stanford University's Asia-Pacific Research Centre; a post doctoral fellow at the University of California's Institute on Global Conflict and Cooperation; lecturer in the department of Political Science and research fellow at the Australia-Japan Research Centre both at the Australian National University.

His publications include "Japan's Strategic Options?", in Purnendra Jain and Lam Peng Er (eds), Japan's Strategic Challenges: China's Rise, the US Hegemonic Decline and Asian Security (Singapore: World Scientific Publisher, forthcoming); "Japan: From Containment to Normalization," in Muthiah Alagappa (ed.) Coercion and Governance (Stanford University

Press, 2001). He earned a Ph.D in Asian and International Studies from Griffith University.

Maj Gen BK Sharma, AVSM, SM** (Retd)

Maj Gen BK Sharma, AVSM, SM** (Retd) is a Distinguished Fellow at the USI. He is PSC, HC, NDC, MPhil (Twice), and PGDM.He is pursuing his PhD in Geopolitics in Central Asia. His prestigious Command and Staff assignments include, Senior Faculty Member at NDC, New Delhi, Command of a Mountain Division, BGS of a Corps, Principal Director Net Assessment, Defence Attaché in Central Asia and UN Military Observer in Central America.

Dr Tuan Yao Cheng

Dr. Tuan Yao is a Research Fellow at the Institute of International Relations (IIR) of the National Chengchi University. He has served in different assignments at the IIR including Director, Deputy Director, Chair of the American and European Research Division, and Chief Editor of America Monthly and Issues & Studies (Chinese edition). He was the visiting scholar at the Pacific Forum – CSIS in 1992, and the George Washington University in 2002-03. His research focus is mainly on American foreign policy, US-China relations, and Asian security.

Shri Ranjan Mathai, Foreign Secretary

Born on May 24, 1952, Shri Mathai joined the Indian Foreign Service in 1974, after completing Post Graduate studies in Political Science at the University of Poona.

He has served in Indian Missions in Vienna, Colombo, Washington, Tehran and Brussels. As Joint Secretary (BSM) in the Ministry of External Affairs in New Delhi (January 1995 to February 1998), he headed the Division dealing with India's relations with Bangladesh, Sri Lanka, Myanmar and Maldives.

He was the Ambassador of India to Israel from February 1998 to June 2001 and to Qatar from August 2001 to July 2005. He next held the post of Deputy High Commissioner of India to the UK in London, from August 2005 to January 2007. He last served as the Ambassador of India to France (since January 2007), with concurrent accreditation to the Principality of Monaco.

Shri Mathai assumed the office of Foreign Secretary on 1 August 2011.

Shri Asoke Kumar Mukerji, Special Secretary

Shri Asoke Kumar Mukerji, is currently the Special Secretary at UN headquarters. He has been appointed as the next Ambassador/Permanent Representative of India to the United Nations at New York.

Other Participants

1. Dr Michael Onderco (Vrije Universities, Amsterdam, Netherlands).

2. Mr Kuang-Chung (Prospect Foundation, Taiwan).

3. Mr Sun Yang-Ming (Prospect Foundation, Taiwan).

4. Ms Yu-Chen Chung (Prospect Foundation, Taiwan).

5. Mr Shih-Wei Yao (Prospect Foundation, Taiwan).

6. Major Ngo Thanh Tung (IDIR, Vietnam).

ACRONYMS

Ser No	Short Form	Full Form
1.	ACFTA	ASEAN China Free Trade Area
2.	ADMM Plus	ASEAN Defence Minister Meeting Plus
3.	ADIC	ASEAN Defence Industry Co-operation
4.	AEC	ASEAN Economic Community
5.	ANZUS	Australia New Zealand United States Security Treaty
6.	APEC	Asia Pacific rim Economic Co-operation
7.	APR	Asia-Pacific-Region
8.	ARF	ASEAN Regional Forum
9.	ASEAN	Association of South East Asian Nations
10.	BMD	Ballistic Missile Defence
11.	CBSS	Council of the Baltic Sea States
12.	CCVI	Climate Change Vulnerability Index
13.	CIER	Chung Hua Institution for Economic Research
14.	CENTO	Central Treaty Organisation
15.	CNOOC	China National Off shore Oil Co-operation
16.	CSCE	Conference on Security and Cooperation in Europe
17.	CTBT	Comprehensive Test Ban Treaty
18.	EAFTA	East Asia Free Trade Agreement
19.	EAS	East Asia Summit
20.	EEZ	Exclusive Economic Zone
21.	FDI	Foreign Direct Investment

22	FMCT	Fissile Material Control Treaty
23.	FTA	Free Trade Agreements
24.	GDP	Gross Domestic Product
25.	GOJ	Government of Japan
26.	GRR	Global Risk Report
27.	IMO	International Maritime Organisation
28.	IOR	Indian Ocean Region
29.	IOR-ARC	Indian Ocean Association for Regional Co-operation
30.	IPR	Indo Pacific Region
31.	ITC	International Trade Centre
32.	JIMEX	Japan Indian Maritime Exercise
33.	JMSDF	Japan Maritime Self Defence Force
34.	KIDA	Korea Institute for Defence Analysis
35.	MPAC	Master Plan on ASEAN Connectivity
36.	NAFTA	North American Free Treaty Area
37.	NATO	North Atlantic Treaty Organisation
38.	ODA	Official Development Aid
39.	OSCE	Organisation for Security and Cooperation in Europe
40.	OVL	ONGC Videsh Limited
41.	PPP	Purchasing Power Parity
42.	PKO	Peace Keeping Operation
43.	RCEP	Regional Comprehensive Economic Partnership
44.	SAARC	South Asian Association for Regional Co-operation

45.	SCO	Shanghai Co-operation Organisation
46.	SEANWFZ	South East Asia Nuclear Weapon Free Zone
47.	SEATO	South East Asian Treaty Organisation
48.	SLOC	Sea Lanes of Communication
49.	SMI	Small and Medium Industries
50.	TAPI	Turkmenistan Afghanistan Pakistan India
51.	TASC	Taiwan ASEAN Study Centre
52.	TPP	Trans Pacific Partnership
53.	UNCLOS	United Nations Convention on Law of Sea
54.	UNCTAD	United Nations Conference on Trade and Development
55.	UNPKO	United Nations Peace Keeping Operations
56.	VPA	Vietnam People's Army
57.	WEF	World Economic Forum
58.	WMD	Weapons of Mass Destruction
59.	WTO	World Trade Organisation

INAUGURAL SESSION

Welcome Address   -   Lieutenant General PK Singh,
                                     PVSM, AVSM (Retd) Director USI.

Keynote Address   -   Ambassador Kanwal Sibal, IFS (Retd)
                                     Former Foreign Secretary

WELCOME ADDRESS

Lt Gen PK Singh, PVSM, AVSM (Retd)

Director, USI

In this, 33rd edition of National Seminar on issues concerning Asia-Pacific-Region we are going to examine Trade, Commerce and security challenges in Asia-Pacific-Region. The Asia-Pacific-Region is dynamic but at the same time complex. The bulk of 21st century history will be scripted here. This region's, strategic and economic importance continues to grow with challenges of reconciling national interests with regional and global interests. Security architecture during Cold-War was based primarily on military analysis. However; today, there is a need to base this architecture on shared values, interests and challenges. We not only need to define but also believe in these universal values. We need to do lot more here, rapid increase in international trade and financial flows, coupled with fiercely competitive MNC's supported by global supply chain networks offer tremendous opportunity for trade and investment. The Asia-Pacific-Region represents 55 per cent of global GDP and 44 per cent of world trade. It is home to some of the largest economies as well as largest militaries. I insist that there is a combination of economics and military strength in this region and that is the reason why we wanted to examine the linkage between these two in our seminar. Security plays a vital role. There is a need to keep transportation network secure and protect the economics and financial infrastructure from attack. We should undertake action to ensure speedy recovery of commerce consequent to foreign attacks and natural disasters.

Despite growing economic integration and strategic dialogue, there still persist distrust and brinkmanship, which can jeopardize peace, stability and economic growth in this region. Hence there is a need to look at linkages between trade, commerce and energy, environment and maritime issues and also the broader linkages between geo-politics, strategy and security. For the question as to why we are trying to do this seminar, linking the issues of trade, commerce and security, I think linkage is very obvious.

This time we shall start talking about the linkages, not about the negatives but the linkages that can be positive, because to say that there is no linkage between trade and commerce would be misrepresentation of the subject. And the second question is, are we looking only at trade and commerce in the context of sale of military equipment? This is just a small part of trade and commerce and not the sole reason. Because, when we consider India's trade with China, we do not have military trade but overall trade is worth, billions of dollars. We are not looking only at the military aspect of trade but the broader connection between trade, commerce and security.

As we are aware there are two sessions today and one session tomorrow, I have no doubt that we will have very stimulating discussions. Once again I thank you all for attending this seminar, I would like to acknowledge the support given to us by the Public Diplomacy Division of Ministry of External Affairs, who are supporting this seminar, who have supported us in earlier events also and we hope they will continue to do so in the future too.

KEYNOTE ADDRESS

Ambassador Kanwal Sibal, IFS (Retd)

Former Foreign Secretary

Impact of geopolitics on trade, commerce, energy environment and maritime issues and their linkages to strategy and security in the Asia-Pacific-Region, is the theme of seminar and I think focus on Asia-Pacific is necessary because global economic, political and military gravity is shifting to this region. Euro-Atlantic region is stable; Africa, however important for natural resources and market forces is not at the centre of fault lines. Latin America also lacks major fault lines. Thus the global implications are in Asia-Pacific.

This region contains most of the population and natural resources much of which lay untapped. The theme of the seminar is very complex as countries have their own understandings and practices of geo-politics depending on geographical locations, neighbours and their relations with each other. In the increasingly globalized and interdependent world, it is difficult to look into issues of Asia-Pacific in isolation. The approaches and possible solutions to challenges that the region faces will be an integral part of the functioning of global system. To start with, we should be clear what Asia-Pacific means?

Asia is land mass and Pacific is water mass. Asia-Pacific is the American geopolitical construct that determines American presence in this extensive stretch. This construct also gives Australia and New Zealand geo-political I-card. How far can we go on the western side of Asia? Do they extend till Iran or go till Turkey. Central Asia would have to be included. Geographical frontiers of Asia pacific are important in defining the challenges and responses of security architecture. They are also relevant in discussing related topics of shared values between Asians. Asia needs to be properly defined and the tendency to limit its western extension till Myanmar to achieve some kind of ethnic coherence needs to be looked into. In any case any ethnic approach to Asia should permit the huge cultural, religious and civilizational impact of India on Asia's eastward expansion. Hence some prominent features of Asia-Pacific need to be spelt out.

To begin with, territorial disputes remain sharp in this region. China claims India's territory and so does Pakistan. Afghanistan has border dispute with Pakistan. China has maritime territorial disputes with Vietnam, Japan, Indonesia, Brunei and Malaysia. Taliban is also involved with them. In the Asia-Pacific construct, western part is Islamic, eastern part is Buddhist. Though there are native Islamic countries like Indonesia and Malaysia, the pacific part is pre-dominantly Christian. Therefore; this region lacks organic religious and cultural unity that today's Europe and America have.

The problem of terrorism is more acute in this region than anywhere else. Border of Pakistan and Afghanistan is the breeding ground for terrorists targeting India and Afghanistan and creating a sense of vulnerability. Nepal, Bangladesh and Sri-Lanka have seen terrorism on their soil; so has China in Xinjiang. Terrorism is a big threat in Indonesia and Myanmar too. This terrorism is largely Islamic, drawing its support from religious radicalism present in this region. The financial and religious linkages of radicalism and terrorism with more conservative Islamic Gulf-countries are real.

Nuclear proliferation is a problem in the two extremities of this region namely Iran and North Korea. On the western side there is a threat from Iran-Israel dispute, despite the possibility of opposition from both Russians and the Chinese. In the case of North Korea, China has opposed any action.

US presence in Asia-Pacific

US presence is substantial in this region with military bases in Japan, South Korea, Thailand, Uzbekistan, Philippines, Afghanistan and Diego Garcia. Some of these countries are military allies of US. Moreover, US 7th fleet is present in this region. There is a consensus about China's rise in the minds of US and its allies; as a result US is strengthening its military presence in this region in the so called rebalancing of Asia. The US defence secretary has described that India is lynchpin of this new strategy. In any case this shows the direction in which US is thinking as far as its partnership with India is concerned. With US 5th fleet and bases in the gulf-region, US has a presence in the western region of Indian Ocean and Strait of Hormuz.

Apart from building pressure on Iran, US claims that this presence is intended to bring stability in the region and bring uninterrupted supply of oil and gas to the friends and allies of US. US imports only 10 per cent of hydrocarbon from this region and its dependency will further decrease due to huge reserves of shale gas discovered in the US. The US has a sizeable presence in the Indian Ocean for ensuring security of the sea lanes of communication. For this it has been engaging in naval exercises on trilateral basis with countries like India-Japan-US.

Analysis of Background paper:

Now your background paper says that security architecture during Cold War was mainly based on military alliances and that there is a need to base this alliance on shared values and challenges. This is likely to be contrary to my views, but some of them can be reiterated, like NATO's role has been expanded and now has a wider geographical reach. For example NATO operated in Yugoslavia, Iraq, and also in Afghanistan and Libya. The US declared its intentions to build military alliances in Asia-Pacific. Russia is also working in Central Asia, bringing deeper security through treaty organisation with previous Soviet states. So, to say that security architecture during Cold War was primarily based on military alliances and that's not the case today is difficult to accept.

This is Euro-Centric view, because China and India and other small countries remain outside Cold-War alliances. The Idea of forming security architecture on shared values is also Euro-Atlantic view. What are the shared values? Are these democracy, human rights, pluralism etc? If we say these are the values, then there are serious differences in these issues. Many countries in the region either do not have democracy or have their own concept of democracy. There is serious opposition for what is seen as American crusade for democracy basically for geo-political reasons. In our tendency to apply this principle, we often over step by using force which results in great human cost. The issue of human rights is highly politicized by the West. Critics believe that it has been used for regime change. There is selectivity in these applications and critics believe that issue has been provocatively used for change.

So can the new security architecture be built on highly contested notions in their practical applications? Can US, Russia and China grow upon a common platform not to mention others like the gulf countries?

India may not have any problem for building such Asia-Pacific construct. Back ground paper also inquires whether India and Pacific Ocean constitute a single strategic space. From my perspective, it is difficult to argue in its favour except from the view point of the US Navy, which has responsibility over both these oceans? In the context of expansion of Chinese blue water Navy, it has the ability to break through chain of Islands and establish increasing presence in the Pacific as well as enter into the Indian Ocean. Two oceans would be considered as a single strategic space. But invariably it seems it is not possible in reality for me. For a country like India that dominates Indian Ocean geographically, would have to contend the entry of Chinese Navy or the way China is creating bases. As regard to the security of sea lanes of communication which is probably the case in Indian Ocean from Strait of Hormuz to Strait of Malacca and Strait of Taiwan to South China Sea but not in the case of Pacific Ocean. Enemy check points across these routes are huge and are vital to economies of Japan, South Korea and China and not to mention India. In this vast stretch there are issues of piracy in Southern Indian Ocean but no sovereignty issues that can threaten international navigation except in South China Sea. All concerned countries that have interest would not interfere in these lanes in the period of tensions because they want to ensure safety. At the moment, two navies which are well placed to ensure this are US and India. Countries like China want independent capacity to do so. This is where geo-political tensions come to play and can be a source of mistrust and problems.

The background paper says that economic issues are the driver of all other issues. I must say this is over stated. Pakistan's hostility towards India is not economic and Nepalese fear about India is also not financial or economic. Terrorism is not driven by economics; radicalization of Islam is not economics. India, China, Japan and Russia's border problems are not economics. US unconditional support to Israel is not economics. Neither are the Israeli policies in its region.

This seminar intends to look at the link between trade and security. There is an international wisdom that more you have trade with the countries there is less number of chances of countries waging war, as the price of war goes up. This could be extrapolated to wider regional canvas of trade linkages and how they act as a buffer against conflict. The evidence to support this on the ground, I think yes to some extent trade and commerce linkages will help to resolve conflict. But when issues involved are such that they are driven by nationalism, countries like to overlook their economic interests and engage in confrontation. China and Japan have large trade and investments but they are involved in political tensions such as the recent Senkaku islands. China and Vietnamese ties are much stronger today, but underlying tensions are real too. Generally speaking China's trade interest in ASEAN region is flourishing like never before. But security concerns have also increased. China has sharpened territorial disputes with ASEAN in the South China Sea. Ideally because of economic growth there will be peace and security, but the same economic growth will lead to increased investments in military. Trade and security can bring peace only if political and territorial issues are resolved.

What is the role of nuclear deterrence? Initially US supported CTBT but now CTBT is off the track. FMCT is not active. Russia and France are against zero-option and Iran and North Korea have thrown up nuclear issues again. Pakistan is expanding its nuclear capabilities and India has to be concerned about it. So deterrence will continue to play a role.

India is energy deficient and non-traditional resources will not help to reduce the dependence on coal drastically. Then water issues are of serious concern due to climate change. Tibet which is major source of water is going to be a major concern, because China is not transparent about it. Bangladesh and India have concerns about it. International co-operation is necessary due to dependence on cyber security. Asia is the engine of world's growth. With diversity, its progress is recognizable but wider Asia-Pacific architecture is difficult to construct as there are several players and diverse conflicting areas. Economics can push for constructing security architecture but it has limited role to play. First countries need to understand on bilateral terms then they have to come together at the multilateral stage that too in a step by step process.

SESSION – 1

TRADE AND COMMERCE IN THE ASIA-PACIFIC REGION AND IT'S IMPACT ON SECURITY

Chairman	-	Dr Daesung Song (ROK)
Co Chairman	-	Major General YK Gera (Retd)
First Paper	-	Mr TC Venkat Subramanian, Ex CMD Exim Bank India
Second Paper	-	Ms Tsun-Tzu Hsu (Prospect Foundation, Taiwan)
Third Paper	-	Cmde Ranjit B Rai (Retd)
Discussion		
Concluding Remarks	-	Major General YK Gera (Retd)

Session -1

Chairman's Opening Remarks

Dr Daesung Song

The topic for the session is "Trade and commerce in the Asia-Pacific-Region and its impact on security". We have three distinguished panelist here and rather than me introducing them I would like to give two minutes to each panelist to introduce themselves. First, I would request Venkat Subramanian, to introduce himself.

Mr. TC Venkat Subramanian

I am Chairman and Managing Director of Export-Import Bank of India (Exim Bank). Prior to this I was the Managing Director and CEO of Exim Bank. I joined Exim Bank of India in 1982 when the Bank was set up. I actively participated in the setting up of Exim Bank as a model public sector organization with a professional work culture.

Ms. Tsun-Tzu Hsu

I am Associate Research Fellow and Section Chief at the Taiwan WTO Centre, and Programme Coordinator at the Taiwan ASEAN Studies Centre (TASC), Chung Hua Institution for Economic Research (CIER), Taiwan (R.O.C). My areas of research include international trade policy and economic/trade law, trade and development issues, regional integration and gender issues.

Cmde Ranjit B Rai (Retd)

I have served as Director Naval Operations (DNO) and Director Naval Intelligence (DNI) at the Naval Headquarters (NHQ). I have served as a Defence Adviser in the Indian High Commission Singapore and South East Asia for four years and have visited Australia, USA and China. I am at present, vice-President of National Maritime Foundation, New Delhi.

Session I

First Paper

Mr. TC Venkat Subramanian, Ex CMD (Exim Bank of India)

Trade and Commerce, in the Asia-Pacific Region and its Impact on Security

Introduction

Trade and Commerce have always remained important factors in determining a country's standing and the political influence it can exert on the global and regional issues. The political influence is derived from the economic strength which is built up through aggressive international trade and commerce. The following chart shows how the world trade has moved over the decades and how the fortunes of the major countries in the Asia-Pacific region have changed :

	1948	1963	1983	1993	2003	2011
Total World Exports (US $ billions)	59	157	1838	3676	7377	17,780
Share of ASIA (in %)	14	12.5	19.1	26.1	26.2	31.1
Of Which						
China	0.9	1.3	1.2	2.5	5.9	10.4
Japan	0.4	3.5	8.0	9.9	6.4	4.5
India	2.2	1.0	0.5	0.6	0.8	1.6
Anz	3.7	2.4	1.4	1.4	1.2	1.6

(Source: WTO/ITC)

India which had a share of 2.2 % of the world trade in 1948, saw its share dwindling steadily, until the trade reforms which were initiated in the 90s, retrieved its position somewhat. However, it is yet to regain the share it had in 1948. Japan also started losing its pre-eminent position it had till early 90s and its share has more than halved over last two decades as also its influence over the region. The star player over the last three decades has been China with its aggressive brand of trade expansion and penetration into all the global markets. Consequently, its influence over the countries in the region has expanded greatly which may become a cause of concern and may also impact the security of some nations.

Global Trade Scenario

Growth in global trade flows slowed down in 2011 due to economic crises in many parts of the world. Still, the overall exports amounted to US $ 17,780 billion as compared to US $ 14,850 billion in 2010. USA, Germany and China accounted for nearly 28 per cent of exports. Asian region including China accounted for 30 per cent of the total exports. In 2011, the top 4 exporting nations were China (US$ 1900 bn with 10.4% share), USA (US$ 1480 bn with 8.1 % share), Germany (US$ 1470 bn with 8.1 shares) and Japan (US$ 823 bn with 4.5 % share). While USA posted a large trade deficit (export minus import) of nearly 700 bn, the other three nations posted trade surplus ranging from US$ 70 bn to US$ 200 bn. India was placed at 19th position with US$ 297 and 1.6 % share.

A significant amount of trade takes place within the region. In the European Union, the intra EU trade is as high as 71 per cent of EU's total exports to the world. Similarly, intra-Asian trade is around 53 per cent of Asia's total exports. Intra- NAFTA exports were around 50 per cent of their total exports. Every country wants to be a dominant player within its region and that may be the reason for increasing intra-regional trade which is more than the inter- regional trade. India's exports to countries in the Asian region (including West Asia) amount to nearly 50 per cent of its total exports. India's exports to countries in Asia-Pacific region alone is about 33 per cent of its total exports.

Asia's Trade Performance

The following chart will illustrate how major Asian countries had performed over last three years which were marked by bouts of economic crises and slowdown in many parts of the world (annual percentage change) :

	GDP			EXPORTS			IMPORTS		
	2009	2010	2011	2009	2010	2011	2009	2010	2011
World	-2.6	3.8	2.4	-12	13.8	5	-12.9	13.7	4.9
Asia	-0.1	6.4	3.5	-11.4	22.7	6.6	-7.7	18.2	6.4
China	9.2	10.4	9.2	-10.5	28.4	9.3	2.9	22.1	9.7
Japan	-6.3	4.0	-0.5	-24.9	27.5	-0.5	-12.2	10.1	1.9
India	6.8	10.1	7.8	-6.0	22.0	16.1	3.6	22.7	6.6
NI Econo-mies	-0.6	8.0	4.2	-5.7	20.9	6.0	-11.4	17.9	2.0

(Source: WTO)

From above chart, it is seen that the performance of Asian region is better than the world, in all three parameters viz. GDP, Exports, Imports. As can be seen, this is primarily due to good performance of both China and India. However, in the year 2012, there has been deceleration in both these economies which may impact the region as a whole.

India's External Trade Performance

India's external trade has been quite buoyant in recent years and the growth rates have been significantly higher, though the imports are still much higher than the exports resulting in sizeable trade deficit. The following chart would give a snapshot of India's external trade over the years:

(US$ BN)	EXPORTS	IMPORTS
1996-97	33.47	39.13
2002-03	52.72	61.41
2007-08	163.13	251.65
2011-12	305.23	489.32

India's exports to Asia-Pacific region in 2011-12 amounted to about US$ 85 billion, equivalent to 28 % of its total exports. Another 22% went to West Asian countries. Thus, India's engagements with Asian nations have been growing in recent years. India has also taken a number of initiatives like its "Look East Policy" to enhance the trade with countries in Asia Pacific region. India's bilateral trade (exports and imports) with Japan has increased from US$ 4 billion in 1996-97 to around US$ 18 billion in 2011-12. India's trade with China, however; increased from US$ 1.3 billion in 1996-97 to a phenomenal US$ 75 billion in 2011-12. But Foreign Direct Investment (FDI) from Japan has been steady and has been to the tune of almost US$ 63 billion over the last decade. FDI from China has been negligible. India's bilateral trade with South Korea in 2011-12 has been around US$ 17 billion. In addition, there are a number of Korean ventures operating very successfully in India.

India vis-a-vis China

India's bilateral trade with China started sometime in early 90s. Initially, China imported more from India than its exports to India, thus giving India a positive trade balance. This position progressively changed over the years and soon the trade balance shifted in favour of China. While China imported mainly raw materials and primary commodities like iron ore from India, its exports were mainly manufactured goods in a number of segments like telecommunication electronics, toys, consumer and industrial products and machinery. As these products were priced very competitively, domestic industrial units, particularly SMI's in these segments started losing out their competitive edge to Chinese firms. The export and import figures in the bilateral trade over the years are captured in the following charts :

YEAR	EXPORTS TO CHINA	IMPORTS FROM CHINA (US$ MN)
1996-97	614	756
2002-03	1975	2792
2007-08	10871	27146
2011-12	18076	57517

(Source: Ministry of Commerce)

Thus, in a span of 15 years the negative trade balance with China has increased from US$ 141 mn to US$ 39441 mn. This trade deficit is almost 22% of the total trade deficit of India for the year 2011-12. This is in spite of the fact that India is considered "less open to trade" than China. "Trade Openness" is measured as "total trade (exports imports) as a % of GDP" of the country. The following chart gives the trade openness of India and China over the decades :

Decade	CHINA	INDIA (%)
1980s	24.7	11.9
1990s	36.6	16.3
2000s	52.3	27.1

(Source: ADB Annual Report)

The above figures indicate that the Indian economy is less integrated with the global economy than the Chinese economy. This is understandable as reforms started in China much earlier (late 70s) as compared to India (early 90s). India's lesser openness to trade and the dominating role of domestic demand, explain why India is barely affected by external shocks compared to China or ASEAN economies.

Issues of Concerns and Impact on Security

Trade and commerce should not normally be a cause of concern or impact a country's internal and external security. But, in current times when trade is used to expand one's sphere of political influence over other countries within or outside the region and to dominate other countries' policies, it becomes a matter of concern. For example, China's aggressive forays into African markets with very cheap trade credits backed by Chinese government agencies, have somewhat dimmed India's age old traditional ties with African nations. The recipient nations are obviously more obliged and favourable to Chinese views than others. The same is the case with Chinese forays into Latin America and South Asia. This could impact India's leadership position in Asia and its close ties with Africa and Latin America. Chinese objection to India's oil exploration agreement with Vietnam is one such example.

China, over the years has emerged as the leading manufacturer and exporter of telecommunication equipment. With an estimated export of US $ 180 billion in 2011, China has overtaken EU as the major exporter of telecommunication equipment to the world. With its unbelievable low cost products, it has made its presence throughout Africa. China exported telecommunication equipment worth US$ 38 billion to USA and about US$ 92 billion to Asian countries last year. Telecommunication equipment is a sensitive item of import which can have security related issues. India has also imported telecommunication equipment from China worth about US$ 7 billion during last two or three years. To quote from the lead article published in a recent issue of the magazine *"The Economist"* of London : " *Huawei, a private firm is a standard bearer in China's long march into Western markets. Its founder , Mr. RenZengfei, who served as an engineer in the People's Liberation Army (PLA), at first struggled to win customers even in*

China......The company is now a US$ 32 billion business empire with 140,000 employees, customers in 140 countries. It commands respect by delivering high-quality telecommunication equipment at low prices. The company is said to be too close for comfort to the PLA. Westerners feel that the networks the firm is building are used by Chinese spooks to eavesdrop during peacetime and could be shut down during war time. They see the firm as a potent weapon in China's burgeoning cyber-arsenal. It is a view that some governments are taking seriously. Earlier this year Australia blocked Huawei's participation in a scheme to build a national broadband network in the country. The company also faced opposition to its commercial expansion in India. And in America, where Huawei's attempts to grow have often been stymied, a congressional committee that focuses on intelligence matters is putting the firm under the microscope; suspicions have been aggravated by a recent spate of cyber-attacks attributed to Chinese hackers." Similarly, a Chinese private firm was recently barred by the US from acquiring four wind mill farms in locations that US considered security sensitive.

Thus, trade and commerce also are subjected to security issues and each country needs to evaluate its own perception of the risks involved in expansion of trade with those countries with whom it had not had best of relations in the past. However, these issues will have to be dealt with caution within the broad framework of World Trade Organisation (WTO) on free flow of trade and commerce. Arguments against imports always need to be viewed with caution, since they will be used by protectionists to keep emerging rivals out, as pointed out by the magazine *"The Economist"* .

Session- I
Second Paper

Ms. Tsun-Tzu Hsu

Trade And Commerce In The Asia-Pacific Region And Its Impact On Security

Introduction

The close economic ties driven by various accelerated integration mechanisms in the Asia Pacific region, particularly among the Southeast and East Asian countries, have contributed significantly to economic growth and shared prosperity in the region in the past decades. Most economies, especially those being benefited from enhanced trade and investment activities with their neighbouring countries believe, economic integration brings positive effects and reduces political and security risks in the region. However, what has happened between China and its neighbouring countries, including Japan and some Southeast Asian countries, in the past months gives the region a lesson that close economic relations with a big neighbour needs more balancing and calculation in order to avoid possible negative consequences.

In the meantime, the Association of the Southeast Asian Nations (ASEAN) proposed to accelerate regional economic integration by developing a Regional Comprehensive Economic Partnership (RCEP) agreement among its 10 member nations and 6 countries which have signed Free Trade Agreements (FTAs) with them, namely China, Japan, South Korea, Australia, New Zealand and India. The major rationale behind the RCEP initiative is the strong political will of the ASEAN to counter balance the US-led trade initiative - the Trans-Pacific Partnership (TPP), and other major powers in the region. Likewise, the initiative also raises the issues of security and stability.

This paper in its first part aims to examine the recently emerging economic tensions or "economic retaliations" of China against some of its trading partners and discusses their policy implications. In the second part, this paper aims to analyze the possible development of the RCEP initiative and tries to assess its impact on the security issues at regional and national level.

The Rise of China and the Two-Sided Effects on the Regional Economy

The rise of China as an economic powerhouse is no doubt an important driving force for the phenomenal economic performance in the East Asia region in the past two decades. Although some countries in the region have been skeptical about China's fast growing economy, political and military influence, no countries have ever tried to refuse the trading opportunities with China. Every country wants to take advantage of China's huge market demands. The ASEAN and China signed the Framework Agreement on Comprehensive Economic Cooperation (ACFTA) in November 2002. The ACFTA was realized on 1 January 2010, since then almost 97 per cent of products classified by ASEAN-6 (Brunei Darussalam, Indonesia, Malaysia, the Philippines, Singapore and Thailand) and China in the Normal Track have been eliminated. The tariffs between the other 4 less developed members, namely Cambodia, Laos, Myanmar and Vietnam, or the CLMV countries, will be fully implemented on 1 January 2015.

According to ASEAN Secretariat statistics, in 2010 China maintained its position as ASEAN's largest trading partner, accounting for 11.3 per cent of ASEAN's total trade, while ASEAN was China's fourth largest trading partner, accounting for 9.8 per cent of China's total trade. ASEAN's exports to China reached US$113.5 billion in 2010, increasing by 39.1 per cent as compared with 2009 and becoming ASEAN's second largest export destination. ASEAN's imports reached US$117.7 billion in 2010, increasing by 21.8 per cent as compared with the previous year. The global financial crisis has made ASEAN more dependent on China as a result of the shrinking demand in the Western countries.

At country level, according to the WTO statistics, in 2010, China is the largest trade partner of Japan, South Korea, Taiwan, and among ASEAN Member Nations, is the largest trade partner of Malaysia and the second or third largest trade partner of several other ASEAN Member Nations. It is also the largest import source of Indonesia, Vietnam and Cambodia, with fast growth in import trade with other Member Nations.

Table 1: China's trade with Asian countries in 2011

	Bilateral trade (US$ 100m)	Growth Rate	Export (US$ 100m)	Growth Rate	Import (US$ 100m)	Growth Rate
Japan*	3,428.89	17.2	1,482.98	22.5	3634.72	14.0
Korea*	2,456.33	15.1	829.24	20.6	1,627.09	17.6
Taiwan*	1,600.32	10.1	351.12	18.3	1,249.20	7.9
India	739.18	19.7	505.43	23.5	233.75	12.1
Indonesia	605.22	41.6	292.22	33.1	313.00	50.5
Malaysia*	900.35	21.3	278.90	17.2	621.45	23.2
Philippines	322.54	16.2	142.54	23.5	180.00	11.0
Singapore	634.82	11.2	355.70	10.0	279.12	12.9
Thailand	647.37	22.3	256.97	30.2	390.40	17.6
Vietnam	402.07	33.6	290.92	25.9	111.16	59.1
Asia	19,030.28	21.5	8,991.42	22.8	10,038.87	20.3
Grand Trade	36,420.58	22.5	18,986.00	20.3	17,434.58	24.9

Source: Ministry of Commerce, China, atvhttp://yzs.mofcom.gov.cn/aarticle/g/ date/p/201202/20120207946820.html.Note: Country market with * has China as the largest trade partner.

On the other hand, according to ASEAN statistics, the foreign direct investment (FDI) flow from China to ASEAN reached US$2.7 billion in 2010, declining by 32.0 per cent from US$3.9 billion in 2009. While according to China's official statistics, accumulative Chinese FDI in ASEAN region has reached US $12.5 billion, nearly half of which was realized in past two years after the global financial crisis.

In addition to trade and investment, tourism is another important sector that has benefited ASEAN economy since China adopted a policy to encourage its citizens to travel overseas, to Southeast Asia. According to ASEAN statistics, in 2010 ASEAN received around 5.4 million tourists from China, increasing by 28.9 per cent as compared with 2009. In 2011, the number of Chinese tourists further reached 7.million, accounting for 9 per cent of total tourists. China has replaced Japan to become the second largest source of tourists for ASEAN, only next to the EU (27). In 2009 China pledged to realize two-way tourist arrivals to 15 million by 2015.

In recent years, China has gradually expanded its official development aid (ODA) and other forms of assistance to ASEAN Member Nations, and has become one of ASEAN's major donors. For example, in 2009 China had initiated US$10 billion China-ASEAN Fund on Investment Cooperation and US$15 billion credit, including US$1.7 billion preferential loans, to support more than 50 major infrastructure development projects in ASEAN Member Nations. The preferential loans were then increased to US$ 6.7 billion. Following adoption of the Master Plan on ASEAN Connectivity (MPAC) in 2009, China again provided an additional US$10 billion credit, including US$4 billion preferential loans and US$6 billion commercial loans to support the implementation of the MPAC. The US$6 billion commercial loans are to be utilized mainly for infrastructure cooperation, energy and natural resource projects.[1]

As a matter of fact, China's huge market demands have not only made her the most desired market in the world, but has also made an increasing number of countries, becoming more and more dependent on Chinese economy for their own economic growth. One important indicator is the Global Risk Report that always attracts a lot of world attention and discussion. According to the Global Risk Report (GRR) released by the World Economic Forum (WEF) based in Switzerland, despite the fact that the rise of Chinese economy has been beneficial to the world economy, it has also become a risk factor in terms of its immediate negative impacts on world economy, especially when its market demands are shrinking.

Based on a comprehensive survey of experts and opinion leaders from around the world, since 2007 the GRR has graded "Chinese economic hard landing" as one of the top global risks on world economy. In 2009

---

[1] The loans are administered by six Chinese banks, namely China Development Bank, China EXIM Bank, Bank of China, Industrial and Commercial Bank of China (ICBC), China Construction Bank and China CITIC Bank.

and 2010, "the Slowing down of Chinese economy (<6%)" was graded in the 2 consecutive years as the second global risk on world economy. These phenomena indicated the increasing dependence of, if not the whole world, a great number of countries, on China both as a major destination of their exports and as an import source of parts and semi-finished materials in supply chains, particularly after the global financial crisis in 2008. This reflects the dilemma these countries are facing. According to a Chinese saying, China to these countries is like "the water", as "the water that bears the boat is the same that swallows it up".

China-Philippines economic relations after the island dispute in April 2012

The rise of Chinese economic influence in the last decades has demonstrated that close economic relations can be a two-sided sword , China can use it to benefit mutual economic and trade ties with other countries on one hand and to "punish" or "retaliate" its counterparts in case of diplomatic stalemate on the other.

One recent example is the China-Philippines relations. China and the Philippines are among the 6 claimants to water and island groups in the South China Sea, which boasts some of the world's most heavily, traveled maritime lanes and rich fishing grounds with a reported potential wealth of mineral resources.

The latest standoff between China and the Philippines began on 10th of April when the Philippine Navy accused Chinese fishing boats of fishing illegally around the Panatag Shoal, otherwise known as the Scarborough Shoal, or in Chinese the Huangyan Island, which the Philippines claimed to have full sovereignty. After the incidents of the dispute, in May China unilaterally suspended various forms of bilateral exchanges and activities with the country, including halting imports from the Philippines that include million tons of bananas, which is the major trade item between the two countries. China also suspended sending Chinese tourists to visit the country and various infrastructures and loans in the Philippines. As a result of China's unilateral actions, business community in the Philippines began to pressurize their government to restore normal relations with China to save their trade and commercial activities.

The issue stemmed from China's rejection of 43 batches of Philippine banana exports over pest infestation issue. The "retaliation" was first reported by banana exporters in Mindanao. China was reportedly imposing tighter rules on banana shipments coming from Mindanao, and rejected some shipments after it allegedly failed in the quarantine tests. Moreover, since May, China's largest travel agent, International Travel Service, has reportedly suspended trips to the Philippines. A similar suspension was ordered by China's nationwide online agency Ctrip.com and the Shanghai Tourism Bureau.

The Department of Trade and Industry (DTI) of the Philippines had first downplayed the increasing inspections by China on Philippine bananas exports as a purely quarantine issue that both parties are trying to settle. However, as China's actions expanded to various sectors, the Philippine government had to respond to Chinese retaliation to save the country's economy.

In 2011, Philippines exports to China reached US$ 18 billion, increasing by 11per cent as compared with 2010. China was Philippines' fifth largest export destination and fourth largest import source. China (including HK) accounts for around 24 per cent of Philippines' total exports. In terms of banana industry, which is Philippines' fifth largest export industry, Japan is the country's biggest export market. Philippines supplies 90 per cent of the Japanese requirement followed by China and the US. In 2011, the Philippines exported a total of $366.68 million worth of bananas to China, supplying more than 92 per cent of its total banana requirements.

On the other hand, China ranks fourth in the country's tourist market. In 2011, a total of 243,137 Chinese tourists visited the Philippines, making it 6.21 per cent of the total arrivals. In the first quarter of 2012 right before the dispute, 96,455 Chinese tourists were received, contributing to 8.4 per cent of the country's tourist market.

Faced with the unexpected retaliation, the Philippine President Aquino had directed concerned agencies to diversify the country's banana exports to cushion the effects of Chinese actions. However, though Philippines bananas have export potentials in other countries such as Australia, Middle East, Russia and Scandinavian countries, the country has to face various challenges, including very high import tariff rates ranging from 10 to 40 per cent, various SPS systems and measures, and high transportation costs, among others.

Relations between claimant countries of South China Sea have soured in 2012. More recently, the island disputes between China and Japan aroused heated responses from Chinese government and made headlines in the world newspapers. Although Chinese government did not officially announce an economic retaliation against Japan, Japan is experiencing suspension of Chinese tourists and a nationwide "Anti-Japanese Campaign" for boycotting Japanese products and services. Ironically, the Chinese leaders have emphasized "the peaceful rise of China" for many years; however, recent disputes between China and its neighbours showed that China might not be so "peaceful" over issues of sovereignty disputes. These incidents also raise the issue that economic integration may have significant impact on national security.

The New Initiative of the RCEP: Will It Address the Security Issue?

Another issue that has caught the world's attention is the accelerated, sometimes overlapping and competing, development of regional economic integration mechanisms in the East and Southeast Asia.[2] These various integration mechanisms or initiatives may lead to positive competition or complication of integration processes, higher transaction costs and increased instability and unpredictability. Most of all, the political wrestling between major economic powers behind various integration mechanisms may very likely give little policy space for smaller economies in the region. Bigger powers may gain more political and economic benefits at the cost of smaller economies.

To counter balance Chinese influence in the region, the Southeast Asian neighbours try to maintain strong bilateral ties with China while in the meantime work towards multilateral arrangements through the ASEAN bloc. A united and strengthened ASEAN has the opportunity to be a player in the region, to deal with China and other bigger countries in the region, such as Japan and Russia, and without, mainly the USA. This strategy can

---

[2] To name some, these include East Asia Free Trade Agreement (EAFTA), based on the ASEAN + 3 and favoured by China and the Comprehensive Economic Partnership in East Asia (CEPEA), based on the EAS and favoured by Japan.

be best demonstrated in the recently proposed integration initiative - the Regional Comprehensive Economic Partnership Agreement (RCEP). Since the US announced its "Pivot to Asia" strategy, the Trans-Pacific Partnership (TPP) has been the Centre of US economic engagement policy in the East Asian region. However, the recently emerging RCEP driven by ASEAN has received growing attention and is regarded as a peer, if not a rival, to the TPP amidst the various integration initiatives. According to the RCEP Framework document released by the ASEAN Secretariat in 2011, the RCEP is planned to include 10 ASEAN Member Nations and their 6 FTA partner countries,[3] and may potentially expand to the US and Russia in the future if the two conduct FTA negotiations with ASEAN.[4] The integration process encompasses a population of 3.5 billion, with its GDP reaching US$ 32 trillion, comprising more than 28.4 per cent of the global GDP and 27.7 per cent of global merchandize trade.

In terms of economic incentives or potential gains, the RCEP may appear to have greater incentives to individual ASEAN Member Nations and their FTA partners. Firstly, the potential economic gains are greater than the TPP, particularly with China and India as potential partners to the RCEP. Secondly, the flexibility of determining different members' liberalization level makes joining the RCEP easier than that of the so called "high standard" trade agreement of TPP. Most of all, the ASEAN-led integration process that will build on the existing FTAs with ASEAN will make negotiations of the RCEP less difficult for both ASEAN Member Nations and those ASEAN+1 countries. According to the ASEAN Secretariat, ASEAN Member Nations in principle have reached a consensus of kicking off negotiations in early 2013; some express their hope to conclude negotiations by 2015 so as to have the RCEP and the formulation of the ASEAN Economic Community (AEC) take place in the same time. (See Table 2)

---

[3] Namely:-China, Japan, South Korea, Australia, New Zealand and India.

[4] Being part of the "ASEAN + 8", the US and Russia were invited to participate in the East Asia Summit and became formal partners in 2012.

Table 2: Comparisons between the TPP and the RCEP

	TPP (P9)	RCEP	
Participants (potential participants)	Singapore, Brunei, Chile, Peru, New Zealand, US, Malaysia, Vietnam, Australia	10 ASEAN member states, China, Japan, Korea, India, Australia, New Zealand	Comparison Not all ASEAN states are TPP members
GDP (% global share)	25.6	28.4	The RCEP, if realized, will become the largest FTA in the world.
Merchandize trade (% global share)	16.3	27.7	
Issues Coverage	Trade in goods, services, investment, trade facilitation, IPR, competition policy, state owned enterprises, government procurement, labour and environment.	Trade in goods, services and investment, customs procedure, technical barriers, IPR, special and differential treatment for less developed ASEAN member states.	The RCEP will not include issues such as competition policy, labour and environment, but will include S&D treatment to less developed ASEAN member states.
Negotiation approach	Single undertaking	Not yet decided	The RCEP may take single undertaking, sequential liberalization or other agreed modality.
Progress	To be concluded by end of 2012.	To start negotiations in early 2013.	The RCEP, based on the 10+1 FTAs, may take less time for consolidation with strong political momentum.
Response from Major Countries	Japan is interested; China, Korea not yet expressed interests.	Japan is interested; China, Korea, India not yet expressed clear interests.	China will join the RCEP to counter balance the US-led TPP; India will also join the RCEP as it is not accessible to the TPP

Conclusion and Policy Implications

The past decade has seen accelerated proliferation of FTAs and RTAs in Asian region. ASEAN has played a key role in driving the economic integration within the region and with external trade partners surrounding the region. There have been overlapping proposals and initiatives such as the ASEAN plus 3, the ASEAN plus 6, East Asia Summit (EAS) and East Asia Free Trade Agreement (EAFTA). The development of the RCEP in the future raises some questions, one of which is whether this ASEAN-led integration process will give ASEAN more economic autonomy and less dependence on big external economic powers, such as China. Given the influence of Chinese economy at regional and national levels, the RCEP or other integration mechanisms will by no means have to face the rising concerns of trade and security along its integration plans. On one hand, the ASEAN Member Nations need China for their economic growth, but on the other hand they also have to live with potential risks in the future that close trade ties with China may turn to have negative impact when political relations sour.

The recent development of China-Philippines relations is a timely example that economic integration and interdependence can be a two-sided sword. When trade is used as a means of retaliation, the WTO or other global trade institutions can hardly provide any effective remedy. How can and should the regional trade architecture, such as the institution of ASEAN and its members, respond and decide collective actions? This will be a difficult issue to tackle.

Session –I

Third Paper

Commodore Ranjit B Rai (Retd)

Trade And Commerce In The Asia-Pacific-Region And Its Impact On Security

Introduction

Trading is an age old phenomenon – the world has indulged in it from time immemorial. Trade means "exchange of one thing for another". Trade is an economic activity. It involves negotiations and then the exchange of one party's goods and services to be transferred and transported/delivered to another. The advent of money as a medium of exchange, and now electronically termed E-Commerce allows trade to be conducted in a manner called 'commerce', this is much simpler and faster in Letters of Credit (L/Cs) and Bills of Lading (B/Ls) compared to earlier forms of trade, such as bartering 'goods for goods', or I Owe You (IOUs). Conventions have been established in trade by UNCTAD. Exchange of currencies and trading in currencies is done by the **Bretton Woods System** of monetary management for commercial and financial relations among the world's major industrial states since the mid-20th century. The Bretton Woods system was the first example of a fully negotiated monetary order intended to govern monetary relations among independent nationstates.

In financial markets, trading can also mean transfers of security and investments, i.e. FDI for foreign direct investment and for internal investment. All these functions are executed between governments, personnel, entities and companies locally and internationally. Nations attach great importance to the overall effect of trade and commerce; hence it has security implications to safe guard and further national interests.

The basic elements of buying and selling in markets have not changed, because ultimately, trade and commerce still involve 'giving and taking and paying' and transportation across boundaries. What has changed is WTO; the World Trade Organization now deals with the global rules of trade between nations to ensure that trade flows fairly and smoothly. The IMO regulations regulate sea transport, as 90% of goods by volume and 75 % by value are transported by sea through the Oceans which is regulated by UNCLOS (1982). Globalization with the help of internet linked nations, companies, finances and people, for movement of information and money. Globalization has impacted the world's trade and commerce system leading to inter-dependence along with security implications, including cyber conflict.

The trade and commercial activities in the 19th century led to colonization by Western nations, weaker and poorer nations lost their sovereign security. China and India leading economies dwindled. In the 20th century trade and commerce was primarily   dominated by the Western nations in monetary terms, political ideas of capitalism, socialism and communism took centre stage in the post-world war period called the Cold War. Trade between one super power block and the other was not easily permitted, and led to security groupings like NATO, WARSAW and military camps. Kautilya has said, "From the economy grows the Army" (Sic... Navy and Air Force). However; the Soviet Union collapsed, as it built up a massive military and its trade and commerce could not support it.

In the 21st century the trade and commerce figures have increased from US$ 12 trillion to US $ 19 trillion. The centre of gravity is shifting towards the eastern side of the Asia Pacific region led by China and India, supplanted by energy export from the Middle East. It has increased reliance on sea transportation, which is the cheapest mode of transport. The majority 60 per cent of the world's goods traverses the Indian Ocean and Indo-Pacific sea lanes.This area has choke points, unsettled land and sea borders and disputes. Hence the subject of trade and commerce is a vital security adjunct which is the subject of this paper with reference to Asia Pacific. Nations protect coastal sea transport by selective Cabotage Law, by not allowing foreign shipping lines the ability to transport goods in coastal trade. India has suffered on this account. India's coastal transport for trade and commerce has not developed.

Rising Economies in the Asia Pacific Region

The Asia Pacific Region is a joint entity of Asia's Eastern land mass, islands in the Indian Ocean and comprises the rising economies of China, India, ASEAN, South Korea and Japan. The region has consistently become the most economically dynamic region in the world and regional economies together account for 44 per cent of world population (2.9 billion people); 40 per cent of global trade ($10.8 trillion) and increasing GDP in purchasing power parity (PPP) terms. As per the World Development Indicators database, World Bank, 1 July 2011, the world's GDP in 2010 stood at US $ 63 trillion.

China became the second largest economy in the world (in PPP terms) with US $ 12 trillion next only to USA at US $ 14.5 trillion, it has overtaken Japan. It is growing at 9per cent mainly through FDI and exports. By comparison, real GDP (PPP) in the rest of the world has only grown at less than 3 per cent per year, and less in recent years. Liberalization, business facilitation, economic mass production by cheap labour in these economies, (especially China) and technical cooperation have helped, economic growth, improve employment opportunities and standards of living for the citizens of the region. There are, however; signs of regional Free Trade Groupings which could also lead to security challenges.

ASEAN as regional grouping has facilitated trade and easy movement of people through co-operation. This co-operation has led to coastal security and states have attacked piracy jointly, the motto 'Eyes in The Sky' is to keep the Malacca Strait open and safe for trade and commerce. Another sign is ASEAN's resolve to write a 'Code of Conduct', to jointly deal with security threats posed by China's strident claims in the South China Sea. China uses its trade and commerce strength and doles, termed 'cheque book diplomacy' to influence nations that have not settled sea boundaries. Recently Cambodia broke ranks with ASEAN on the 'Code of Conduct'. Soon nations will have extended EEZ from the current 200nm. Their claims on the continental shelf can lead to conflicts.

An active trade grouping in the region is the Asia Pacific Rim Economic Co-operation (APEC) with ASEAN, Japan, Russia, Canada and USA. Its Economic and Technical Cooperation (ECOTECH) activities are designed to build capacity and skills in APEC member economies at both the individual and institutional levels and to participate more in the regional economy. Since APEC first began to undertake capacity building work in 1993, around 1600 projects have been initiated. APEC contributes funding to around 100-150 projects each year, with a total value of over $23 million committed by APEC to projects in 2010-2011. This focus is reducing the digital divide between the industrialized and developing economies.

South Asian Association for Regional Co-operation (SAARC) has not been successful in trade due to security challenges between India and Pakistan. It was Admiral TeoCheHean the current Deputy Prime Minister of Singapore who always advocated, "A benign strategic relationship and understanding between nations is essential for trade and commerce". This theme can explain in brief the security challenges in Asia Pacific which will show how Singapore has built up a co-operative relationship with India. Singapore is an important trading partner of India with bilateral trade of about US $ 6.4 billion. It ranks first in terms of India's bilateral trade in the ASEAN region. The balance of trade has traditionally been in favour of Singapore. Imbalance can also pose challenges.

The Impact on Security

If there is no growth through trade and commerce, there will be no stability. If there is no substantial consumer and consumption growth in these economies, there will not be stability, and instability leads to conflict. If a nation cannot get the resources and they see insufficient rules set to guarantee them by import then there will be conflict. China and India with large populations need energy and food resources in large quantities hence a competition in trade and commerce for resources will follow. Whilst most Asia Pacific countries are low on GDP they are bound to rise. Nations that invest will look for stability and a return on their investment. This paper states that if nations do not have sufficient political and military security and benign strategic understandings these rules would not emerge. The US with a pivot in the East believes that if there is no military leviathan in Asia-Pacific, the region will not have such security and stability and the US Navy believes it has a substantial role in this regard. China does not welcome such moves. She has claims on islands on historical grounds, for resources and control of sea trade. Colin Gray does predict a bloody century. If his and Mahan's predictions that the future of the world will be decided on the waters of the Indian Ocean in the 21st Century comes true, then Americans and European Union have strategic understanding and threats are low. The threats with nuclear powers like China, Pakistan, North Korea and India and aspiring Iran are in this region. Security threats can break into trade wars and conflict.

This brings the paper to sea transportation and in this age of globalization; nations will need maritime power to ensure safety of sea lanes for trade and commerce and the 21st century is beginning to become the century for Maritim-ization. Navies in the Asia Pacific region led by China and India with 45 warships are already leading the pack. China's economy can support the growth.

Conclusion

Many things happen when governments fail in their efforts to manage the macroeconomic and security environment. First, government credibility is undermined and the effectiveness of security is closely linked to government credibility, the equivalent of political capital that should never be wasted. Beyond issues of credibility, poor management of public resources limits choices and curtails the ability of government to respond to the most pressing needs, such as education, training, research and development. As a consequence, countries fall behind with respect to others, and catching up, if it can be done at all, requires extra effort and expenditure of greater resources than would have been necessary in the presence of good policies.

Session-I : Discussion

Issue Raised

What is the difference between TPP and RCEP? Is Japan interested to join RCEP and what is the South Korean view point about this? How can RCEP play a role to change the landscape?

Responses

(a) TPP is out of fashion in the Asia-Pacific-Region. RCEP is proposed by ASEAN and it wants to be in the driver's seat; so in this region RCEP will dominate. ASEAN in its website has updated what RCEP is going to do in the future. Due to RCEP India and China can do FTA negotiations. China does not have problems with RCEP as United States (US) is not included.

(b) South Korea cannot disregard security issues and hence it is difficult to ignore TPP. At the same time due to economic reasons they would like to associate with RCEP also.

Issue Raised

There is an increase in trade between China and Taiwan. How does Taiwan view this situation? Will it be to Taiwan's advantage?

Response

There is a lot of interaction between China and Taiwan because of similar culture, language and business interests. Though Taiwan's exports to China are more; imports from China to Taiwan are also increasing. Consequently Taiwan wants to have trade with other countries like Russia, Brazil and India.

Issue Raised

India has trade deficit with China, while Taiwan has surplus. Is there any relation between trade balance and security?

Responses

(a) If trade is balanced, then conflicts can be reduced. Imbalance in trade increases the chances of conflict.

(b) Trade imbalance can make China aggressive. Past records show that Chinese rulers had banned Philipino bananas and restricted Chinese from visiting Philippines thus affecting their tourism. These were the main sectors of economy of Philippines and they were hampered severely.

Issue Raised

What can India do to ensure security as trade and commerce grows?

Response

Maritime trade and commerce is growing. India can help to bring order in Maritimization.

Issue Raised

Can South Korea and Japan come together to counter a rising China?

Response

There are historical factors for rivalry between South Korea and Japan. There are territorial disputes. It is difficult to predict anything at present.

Issue Raised

How trade is used to punish each other, are there any networks like EXIM banks which are involved in these activities?

Response

These networks are not autonomous and do not have any legal sanctions. In trade negotiations principle of 'might is right' still prevails.

Session -I
Co-Chairman's Concluding Remarks
Major General YK Gera (Retd)

Historically there was a time when "Might was Right" but today the situation has changed. Today economic development can take place only when assurance for security is there. At the same time without economy military power cannot be sustained. Environment has gained importance and it needs to be secured. In today's world both economy and security are important. Internationally there is a need for synergy between the economic structures and security structures. I thank the panelists who have tried to connect the impact of economy on the security of Asia-Pacific Region.

SESSION – II

ENERGY, ENVIRONMENTAL AND MARITIME SECURITY

Chairman	-	Vice Admiral PS Das, PVSM, AVSM, VSM (Retd).
First Paper	-	Dr. Annika Bolten-Drutschmann.
Second Paper	-	Vice Admiral Arun Kumar Singh, PVSM, AVSM, NM (Retd).
Third Paper	-	Sr Col Le Kim Dung
Fourth Paper	-	Mr. Ivan Safranchuk
Discussion		
Concluding Remarks	-	Vice Admiral PS Das, PVSM, AVSM, VSM (Retd).

Session - II

Chairman's Opening Remarks

Vice Admiral PS Das, PVSM, AVSM, VSM (Retd)

I would like to thank USI for giving me this opportunity to chair the session. I would not take much time in introducing the speakers. I hope the bio-datas of the speakers are available with everyone. I would request the speakers to start the session. The first speaker would be Dr. Annika Bolten-Drutschmann, Policy Planning Staff, Federal Foreign Office, Germany.

Session - II

First Paper

Dr. Annika Bolten-Drutschmann

Maritime Security in Asia: Lessons From Europe?

Introduction

Maritime security will probably be the defining issue for Asia's geopolitical and security architecture in the 21st century. Indeed, many, if not all, of Asia's geopolitical hotspots, historical enmities and unresolved territorial disputes concern maritime zones. The resulting strategic uncertainty has been further heightened by growing military spending over the course of the last decade generating a significant disruptive potential for the global economy and global peace and stability. Therefore, the aim of this panel, that is *"to suggest ways and means to evolve an open, transparent and inclusive maritime security structure and to facilitate maritime security cooperation"* is a very timely one.

This paper seeks to combine two aims. First, building on a brief analysis of the current state of the regional security architecture in Asia, it seeks to draw on the European experience of overcoming the Cold War divide and dealing with maritime security issues with focus on the Baltic Sea and the *Conference on Security and Cooperation in Europe* (CSCE). Secondly, based on these lessons, the paper outlines potential contributions by the European Union to facilitate the emergence of an open, transparent and inclusive security structure in Asia.

In a nutshell, the thesis put forward argues that Europe's experiences of dealing with and ultimately overcoming Cold War tensions suggest that the "old continent" has much more to offer than trade and investment to today's Asia. Indeed, the question is: How can we make best use of this expertise and experience in light of today's security challenges in Asia? After all, there is and will be no single recipe for global peace. Nor can the

European experience simply be replicated in Asia. Yet, the experiences of the process of the CSCE may offer useful starting points for jointly building confidence and strengthening the security architecture among Asian nations. Therefore, even in times of great scrutiny of the "European project" at home and abroad, Europe has a relevant contribution to make in this context – and has itself much to gain from a stable and strong Asia. This message needs to be better understood – both in Asia and in Europe.

A Regional Security Architecture in Asia

Former Australian Foreign Minister Kevin Rudd, stated that we witness *"[a] 21st century Asian economy resting on the shoulders of a 19th century set of security policy realities"*.[i] Indeed, to date, a stable and effective system of collective security in Asia is yet to emerge. Instead, a unique and complex but yet overall weak web of multilateral and bilateral agreements and security partnerships, networks and dialogue processes ranging from ASEAN and the ASEAN Regional Forum (ARF) to the East Asia Summit (EAS) seeks to address the manifold security issues in the region.

In turn, the challenges, which this security web is meant to address, are fast growing. Military spending is on the rise across Asia.[ii] Nationalisms are becoming politically more visible, vocal and influential not only in China, but also in Vietnam, Philippines and elsewhere. Analysts speak of an increasingly fragile security environment, which could progressively be destabilized by isolated incidents and escalating territorial disputes – often in maritime areas. China and India, as the two major rising powers in Asia, are increasingly becoming maritime powers, whilst archipelago nations such as Indonesia and the Philippines have set themselves ambitious goals for modernising and expanding their respective navies. Asian powers are increasingly interested in the wider oceans beyond their shores. This shift coincides with a time when the security environment in Asia in the aftermath of the US "rebalancing towards Asia" is increasingly seen through the prism of a US-China rivalry. Whilst China is becoming increasingly assertive, the US has once more underlined its role as a key actor in regional stability in Asia given its long-standing security commitments to Japan, South Korea and Taiwan as well as to certain ASEAN member states. Similarly, rising energy demands and the desire for greater energy security is ushering an intensified competition for resources, more broadly, which may compound maritime tensions in the region and thus may contribute to even greater uncertainty in maritime security.

This fragile security climate constitutes a significant threat to the mid-term global political ambitions of Asian countries and their continued economic development and prosperity. The last few decades suggest that bilateral solutions to territorial disputes and historical enmities are unlikely to emerge in the short run. Yet, to date, a multilateral regional security architecture resembling that of Europe with confidence-building measures, arms control regimes, disarmament schedules and other forms of security cooperation in a multilateral setting remains but a distant vision. Indeed, sustainable multilateral security structures in Asia are only to emerge, if the "big" players in the Asia-Pacific-Region regard such structures to be in their national interest. This, to date, is not the case. Muddling through and pursuing national interests through bilateral negotiation processes appears to be a more attractive option, especially for China.

In contrast, however, we increasingly witness a growing awareness and interest especially by the "middle powers" in the region and regional organizations, such as ASEAN, in organizing a more efficient web of security relationships for instance, strengthening the existing frameworks of the ARF and the EAS. The aim of such efforts is to build a regional architecture that creates binding and sustainable rules that entangle all parties involved and thus (re-)generate the degree of confidence that arguably has been lost lately. ASEAN is seeking regional resilience in a security structure centring on ASEAN. In order to avoid becoming a hayfield for outside powers. These efforts could gain in substance by engaging in a more sophisticated manner with the European experience in the context of the CSCE.

The European Cold War Experience: A useful starting point

Peace and stability in Asia also remains a key foreign policy goal both for the European Union and of its individual member states.Perhaps more than ever before, Europe relies on markets and supplies from Asia. The implications of potential instability in maritime security relations in Asia for the EU and indeed for the entire world are, therefore, considerable. With almost 90 per cent of the EU's external trade by sea and Europe's economy becoming increasingly integrated with Asia, Europe's future growth and prosperity will increasingly become contingent not only on Asia's economic development but also on a politically stable Asian region and open sea lanes. Concerns about piracy and human trafficking on sea routes only serve to compound this interest in maritime security in Asia.

Europe thus possesses a real and legitimate interest in actively contributing towards processes that bolster stability and security cooperation in Asia. In this vein, in its recently issued "Guidelines on the EU's Foreign and Security Policy in East Asia" (approved on 15 June 2012), the EU states that "the embedding of political and security cooperation among the region's major players will be of great benefit for the region as a whole, and is something which the EU must continue to support actively".[iii] In practical terms, this implies an enhanced EU effort as under:-

(a) Promote confidence-building measures and conflict resolution methods in Asia.

(b) Encourage greater transparency in defence expenditure through, among other measures, military-to-military exchanges.

(c) Share lessons drawn from its own experiences of post-war reconciliation, confidence-building and preventive diplomacy."[iv]

The guidelines display a healthy realism on the part of the EU. Indeed, given its limited leverage in Asia, it is unlikely that the EU will become a lead player in Asian maritime security in the short and medium run. Yet, given its projection as a neutral power in Asia, the EU could be doing much more to systematically encourage solutions on the basis of its considerable "soft" power without running the risk of "overstretching". Europe's experience of seeking to achieve transparency, to build confidence and to organize cooperation across the Baltic Sea during the complicated transition from a zone of confrontation to an area of potential cooperation and indeed integration serves as an example of the wider CSCE process, which appears to be most relevant in this context.

The CSCE Experience: Model for a Conference for Security and Cooperation in Asia

The CSCE, one of the main elements in bringing about the "New Europe" after the end of the Cold War and still in existence today as the *Organization for Security and Cooperation in Europe* (OSCE), holds a treasure trove of institutional solutions, procedures and personal experiences which may be worth looking at in the quest for a sustainable and all-encompassing Asian security structure. The convening of the CSCE – a diplomatic conference among 35 participating states that served a multilateral forum for dialogue and negotiation between the East and West – was made possible by a consensus that emerged in the early 1970s.

The CSCE's bold gamble, the farsightedness of the diplomats, to convince their political masters to sit down at the same table "with the enemy" showed the CSCE's conflict and crisis managerial role. Against the background of the Soviet crushing of the Prague spring (1968), East and West had eventually come to the conclusion that only truly multilateral action could pull Europe back from the brink of another major military confrontation. The CSCE process allowed countries, which did not, at least initially, officially recognise each other (e.g., the German Democratic Republic (GDR) and the majority of Western countries) to meet on a routine basis to talk, size each other up and thus develop a dialogue and transparency rather than un-reflected menace. A fortunate historical circumstance meant that the "heavy burden" of negotiations was addressed in parallel negotiations of the Non-Proliferation Treaty (1968), the Strategic Arms Limitation Treaty talks between the Soviet Union and the US (1969) and the Mutual and Balanced Force Reduction talks between NATO and the Warsaw Pact. The CSCE could, therefore, become a genuine conference for the future, rather than being burdened by the past.

After the conclusion of its core document, the so-called "Helsinki Final Act", in 1975, the CSCE process had several characteristics, which may also appeal to today's Asia. First, it was as democratic a conference between unequal participants as was institutionally possible. All parties had the same rights. Decisions were reached by consensus. Every party was free to bring its ideas and proposals to the negotiating table. Secondly, process was kind. At no point was process constrained by pre-ordained structures. Indeed, the CSCE was always considered to be a work in progress. The "Helsinki Final Act" never had the ambition to become a legally binding treaty but it was signed at the highest level by each participating state and thus carried a moral commitment by each party both towards the outside world and its own citizens.[v] Thirdly, the CSCE was arguably the first forum where the term "confidence building measure" (CBM) was first coined. At first exclusively used for military negotiations, it was an elegant admission that some hard security facts could not be negotiated away but could nevertheless be "softened" by making them more visible, explicit and thus more predictable. Following this logic, CBMs were introduced into other areas, like the very delicate fields of human rights and humanitarian policy. Fourthly, with the commitment of the participating parties to a set of core principles in the fields of politico-military, economic, environmental and human rights issues, as its sound foundation and a shared expectation that there would always be a next meeting, the "Helsinki process" was able to survive the highs and lows in East-West relations. The broad network of contacts across the 'Iron Curtain', fostered through specialized conferences and expert meetings; a wide range of issues. The process-oriented nature of the CSCE also proved a key in adapting to changing political circumstances in the aftermath of the collapse of the Soviet Union and the fall of the Iron Curtain. Through its norm-creating and monitoring functions, the CSCE steered developments into a positive direction and reduced uncertainty during this difficult transition phase. Finally, in 1992, the CSCE became the *Organization for Security and Cooperation in Europe* (OSCE) with a consensus-minus-one rule, permanent structures and a headquarters in Vienna.[vi] Since its 2010 Astana Summit, the OSCE pursues a new strategic vision encompassing novel threats to security, such as terrorism, organised crime and drug or human trafficking and enshrining its commitment to greater engagement with other regional organisations, including those in Asia.

The case of the Baltic Sea

In the context of maritime security the case of the Baltic Sea is of particular relevance. Indeed, today, the Baltic Sea is one of the most heavily shipped seas in Europe and remains a key for Europe's energy security (e.g., North Stream pipelines). Bordered by currently nine littoral states, of which Russia is the only non-EU member state,[vii] the Baltic Sea constituted the borderline between the two opposing systems during the Cold War period. Interaction across the Sea was limited. The Region was characterized above all by political and military tensions. Indeed, given Russian capabilities, which exceeded those in the region and were only checked by over-the-horizon capabilities of the US, there was never any real military "balance" in the region during the period of the Cold War. In short, for much of the

Cold War the Baltic Sea was an area of negative peace characterised by the absence of war but also an acute lack of positive cooperation.[viii] The notable exception to this rule – and ultimately a key experience for post-Cold War efforts at establishing greater cooperation across the Baltic Sea – was the *Baltic Marine Environment Protection Commission* (HELCOM) set up in 1974, which grew, out of maritime pollution concerns shared by the then seven coastal Baltic Sea states.[ix]

The rapprochement in the context of the CSCE brought about considerable benefits in terms of greater predictability and confidence in the Baltic Sea context – and it provided a key normative framework for addressing the key questions raised in the immediate aftermath of the collapse of the Soviet Union, such as the procedures for the pull-out of Russian troops from the Baltic states in 1994-5 and for ensuring the protection of the rights and freedom of the resulting Russian minorities.

The framework also shaped the context in which new regional organisations and cooperation frameworks at various levels emerged to fill the vacuum across the Baltic Sea and established themselves as central forums for fostering trust and confidence, such as the *Council of the Baltic Sea States* (CBSS) 1992, which in addition to the nine littoral states also includes Norway and the European Commission.[x] The CBSS, organised in three working groups, enshrined a strong commitment towards soft and civil security issues such as the promotion of nuclear and radiation safety, the continued building of regional confidence through the promotion of democracy and human rights, the facilitation of trade and investment across borders by dismantling trade barriers and promoting twinning agreements. Today, the Baltic Sea has become a sea of cooperation and has left its history of divisions largely behind.

This historical sketch of the European experience with the CSCE process and its impact for the Baltic Sea does not pretend to suggest that Asia would or should follow a similar path towards in-depth institutionalisation, nor that the evolution of a temporary conference process into a regional organisation is *per se* desirable. Rather, the European CSCE experience suggests that pragmatism and the presence of multilateral, all-encompassing structures where regional problems and challenges can be discussed and debated are useful starting points when reflecting on future security structures in Asia.

Options for the European Union and Asia in Strengthening Maritime Security

The EU should, therefore, use its perception as a "neutral broker" in Asia more effectively with respect to encouraging cooperative security solutions, based on international law. Indeed, greater efforts to strengthen the regional security architecture are ultimately in the interest of all our Asian partners, for the rising major powers as much as the middle powers. Stability and confidence, after all, are key preconditions for continued economic growth and prosperity.

More concretely, what could and should the EU, therefore, do with respect to facilitating the emergence of an open, transparent and inclusive maritime security structure in Asia? Upon request and on the understanding, that the European way can only be an inspiration and not a blueprint for Asia, the EU should strengthen partnerships built around its main asset in this context, which is soft power along the lines of the expertise acquired over the years in the processes described above. Such engagement would be particularly effective if embedded in a wider inter-regional framework such as the EU's membership of the ARF. Therefore, the EU should do the following:-

(a) Provide greater technical assistance and legal expertise to strengthen regional processes, such as the ARF Secretariat based on the ASEAN Secretariat in Jakarta, and to help facilitate the transitioning of the ARF from its initial focus on CBMs to preventive diplomacy in the context of its PDWork Plan.

(b) Engage more actively with the *ARF Inter-Sessional Meeting on Maritime Security* [xi] and offer, once more, the sharing of expertise and best practices concerning the joint management of maritime resources and fisheries policies.[xii]

(c) Exchange views on best practices in the field of environmental protection and the joint preservation of biodiversity in maritime areas as informed by the experience of the HELCOM.

(d) Intensify its engagement with the *EU-ASEAN Experts Group Meeting on Maritime Security*, with a view to cooperate more closely in combating piracy as well as other trans-national crimes, including trans-national/maritime terrorism.

(e) Continue its efforts to intensify relations between the ARF Unit and the OSCE Secretariat as well as to deepen the level of political dialogue and contacts between the OSCE and ARF.

Ultimately, given the rise of the EAS as increasingly the core institution of common security in Asia, the EU ought to hold on to its goal of obtaining membership in this new grouping. Uniting the *"ASEAN plus Eight"*, that is the ten ASEAN member states, Japan, China and Korea (the so-called "Plus Three") as well as Australia, New Zealand and India ("Plus Six"), Russia and the United States, the EAS' membership is also replicated in the new format of the *"ASEAN Defence Ministers Meeting Plus (ADMM Plus)"*.[xiii] This does not undermine the argument in favour of a stronger engagement with the ARF. On the contrary, a more substantial European contribution to Asian security in the context of the ARF may, therefore, bring a greater regional relevance than what we have witnessed to date. This may indeed be what the EU needs to substantiate, its membership application to the EAS.

Concluding Remarks

Germany is one of those European nations that experienced the benefits of confidence and security building measures in its recent history in a major war. Insurmountable walls and barbed wires, fear and threat were ultimately overcome by consistent and persistent efforts to create trust and transparency. This experience and the interest-based awareness of the very real costs of escalating conflicts in Asia, be it maritime or anything else, for Germany (its economy), as well as those of its neighbours combine to form a strong commitment towards seeking to contribute, where requested, to regional efforts that strengthen the Asian security structures and make military conflict less likely.

This has strongly encouraged the EU, to generally enhance its strategic partnerships in Asia and its political presence on the Asian stage. It has, in addition, also taken the form of German initiatives within the ARF framework and embedded in the EU context, which aim at promoting exploratory exchanges between the OSCE and the ARF, to enhance all parties' understanding of confidence-building measures and preventive diplomacy.[xiv]

Future initiatives may centre on a co-chaired seminar on stockpile management, export and border controls with particular emphasis on MANPADS (Man Portable Air Defence Systems) and expert workshops on CBMs in global cyber-security.

The message is clear: Germany believes that Europe and the European Union has a contribution to make to foster the emergence of an open, transparent and inclusive security structure in Asia and a very particular and unique one at that. Yet, for this message to be transmitted to Asia, greater and a more visible and consistent engagement in the field of foreign and security policy on the part of the EU is necessary. Finally, given that, as US Secretary of State Clinton said in Vladivostok in September 2012, *"much of the history of the 21st century is being written in Asia"*, let us hope that our Asian partners will not repeat the mistakes that were made in interwar Europe and let their choices be informed by the tough historical lessons the European people had to learn.

References

i.   Address to the North Atlantic Council of NATO by (then) Foreign Minister Kevin Rudd in Brussels, Belgium on 20 January 2012.

ii. SIPRI quotes an increase in the Chinese defence budget by 6,7% p.a. to a 2011 budget amounting to approx. 143 billion US$. However, increases in military spending have also been noted for, among others, India, Vietnam and Indonesia as well as Russia. Only the rate of increase in military budgets on the African continent exceeds the growth rate in Asia.

iii. Council of the European Union (2012), *Guidelines on the EU's Foreign andSecurity Policy in East Asia*, http://eeas.europa.eu/asia/docs/guidelines_eu_foreign_sec_pol_east_asia_en.pdf, p. 8.

iv. Ibid, p11.

v.   In terms of "process", the CSCE also differentiated itself from other conference settings by keeping, with a few exceptions, all CSCE deliberations confidential. No official summary was ever made, no joint official press conferences were held. Instead, media had to rely on individual briefings by participating countries.

vi. The Helsinki Summit in 1992 declared the OSCE to be a regional organisation under Chapter 8 of the UN Charter.

vii. The states bordering on the Baltic Sea are: Russia, Finland, Sweden, Denmark, Germany, Poland, Lithuania, Latvia and Estonia. Norway is sometime also referred to due to its membership in the Council of the Baltic States.

viii. Some may want to argue that the Finno-Soviet relationship represented an exception of sorts.

ix. The HELCOM convention ultimately entered into force in 1980 and was revised in 1992 in light of the political changes in the region. Since then, its permanent secretariat in Helsinki implements the members' joint commitments in terms of environmental protection and the drafting of regional laws in this field.

x. To give a few examples: At governmental level, the Council of Baltic Sea States (CBSS) was founded in 1992. Parliamentarians established the Baltic Sea Parliamentary Conference (BSPC) in 1991. In 1993, the sub-regions founded the Baltic Sea States Sub-regional Cooperation (BSSSC) and the cities of the Region formed the Union of Baltic Cities (UBC) in 1991.

xi. The 5th Meeting of the ARF ISM is scheduled for April 2013 in the Republic of Korea.

xii. The offer of sharing experiences from the Baltic Sea and the Mediterranean Sea to ASEAN as a regional organization has been on the table since the EU-ASEAN SOM in Warsaw in November 2011. Due to internal divisions, no uptake has been forthcoming to date.

xiii. In contrast to the ARF circle, this grouping unites a more limited number of more influential countries making it a more substantive forum of choice for discussing strategic issues such as the South China Sea.

xiv. The latest edition of this exchange in the ARF context took place in Berlin in November 2011 under the co-chairing of Germany (on the part of the EU) and Indonesia (on the part of ASEAN).

Session - II
Second Paper

Vice Admiral Arun Kumar Singh, PVSM, AVSM, NM (Retd)
Maritime Challenges in the Asia Pacific Region

Though modern strategic thinkers see the Asia Pacific Region (APR) and the Indian Ocean Region (IOR) as one entity called the Indo-Pacific Region (IPR), this paper deals specifically with Maritime Challenges in the APR.

The APR (along with India) is economically the fastest growing region in the world, and encompasses some very rich nations (which primarily need the sea for exporting their goods, and also for importing energy and raw material) like Japan, China, South Korea, Taiwan, Australia etc along with other growing powers like Vietnam, Philippines, Indonesia, Malaysia, Brunei etc. Just north of Japan and South Korea lies oil and gas rich Russia, which has a dispute with Japan over a few islands. Russia, apart from being a major energy exporter, also is a major arms supplier to China, Vietnam and India. India, which has oil exploration rights in Russia's Sakhalin Island, has also been invited by Vietnam to explore oil in its waters, located in the SCS. Freedom of navigation at sea and safety of SLOCs is vital to India, since 50% of its seaborne trade goes eastwards to the APR.

The APR comprises the East Asian land mass, numerous islands, and disputed waters via Yellow sea, East China sea (ECS), South China sea (SCS). Amongst all the nations comprising the APR, perhaps China is geographically the most disadvantaged. Despite having the world's fastest growing economy, navy and merchant marine, backed by 52 major seaports and 16 major inland river ports, and despite having a massive shipbuilding industry, its seaward movement eastwards into the Pacific ocean can be locked by three island chains, whilst its seaward movement into the IOR can be blocked at the straits of Singapore-Malacca, Sundae and Lombok. Access to the north eastern APR can be controlled by three Japanese controlled straits viz Osumi, Tsushima and Tsugaru. The two major SLOCs are SCS to IOR, Middle East and beyond; ECS, Sea of Japan, to Pacific ocean, USA and Canada.

The SCS is strategically located for controlling SLOCs, while its 3 million sq kms contain an estimated 50 million tons of oil, huge reserves of gas, mineral wealth and fish. 25% of global crude passes through the SCS. The oil tanker traffic is three times more than Suez Canal and five times more than Panama Canal.

The SCS has hundreds of tiny islands and reefs which are under dispute, primarily as their control gives large EEZ which can then be exploited for energy, minerals and fishing. These disputes have the potential of erupting into war, and can disrupt innocent seaborne commerce, which already faces the threats of sea piracy and maritime terror. In addition, if a powerful nation like China can convert the SCS into its territorial waters, it will have serious ramifications on freedom of navigation at sea for the international seafaring community.

After the 1974 naval clash between China and Vietnam, all the Paracel group of islands are under Chinese control. The claimants for the over two hundred Spratly islands are China, Taiwan, Malaysia, Vietnam, Philippines and Brunei. All the claimants except Brunei are presently in occupation of some islands, with Vietnam in occupation of the largest number i.e. 20 islands.

Disputes in the APR have been ongoing for a few decades as shown below –

- On 19 January 1974, a naval clash took place off the Paracel islands between China and Vietnam. After this, China was in occupation of all the Paracel group of islands.

- On 14 March 1988, a naval skirmish took place off Johnsons reef (Spartly) between Vietnam and China. After this incident China was in occupation of 8 islands Out of the over 200 islands of the Spratly group.

- On 16 May 2009, China imposed a summer fishing ban in the SCS, and sent ships to enforce the ban, overriding Vietnamese protests about violation of its traditional fishing rights. It may be noted here, that despite modern territorial waters being 12 nautical miles (nm), French fishermen are permitted within six nm of the British coast.

- On 05 January 2010, China announced tourism packages to some of the disputed islands in the SCS.

- On 09 February 2010, China announced new oil and gas finds in the disputed SCS, while Japan went in protest to an International maritime court, against a similar Chinese "finds"   in the ECS.

- On 26 March 2010, the 1200 ton South Korean Navy corvette the Cheonan was sunk by a torpedo in the Yellow sea. Apparently the attack was carried out by a North Korean mini submarine, in retaliation for earlier naval clashes between the two navies in the Yellow sea, in 1999, 2002 and 2009, where the North Koreans took a beating.

- On 7 Sep 2012, a Chinese fishing boat collided with Japan Coast Guard (JCG) patrol boat, in the vicinity of the disputed Senkaku (Diaoyu) islands, which are presently under Japanese control.

- In June 2012, the Vietnamese government announced that it had passed a law, claiming sovereignty over all the Parcel and Spratly islands. In July 2012, the Chinese responded by announcing the creation of "Sasha city" in one of the Paracel islands, which has population of 159 civilians, in addition to a Navy and Army garrison. Water and food for this total population of about 800 people is supplied regularly by ships of the Chinese Navy.

- The APR has a number of disputes which are enumerated below:–

  - In the ECS, China, Japan and ROK (South Korea) are involved in an EEZ dispute.

  - In the ECS, China, Taiwan and Japan are involved in a dispute over the eight Senkaku (Diaoyu) islands, which are presently under Japanese control.

  - Japan and China have a dispute over Okinotori-Shima islet, while Japan and South Korea have dispute over Liancourt (Takeshima) Rocks.

- In the SCS, disputes over 200 islands involve, China, Taiwan, Vietnam, Malaysia, Philippines, Indonesia and Brunei.

- In the Yellow sea, dispute over the maritime delineation line has resulted in naval clashes and artillery bombardment between North and South Korea.

The global maritime community faces some common challenges in the APR. These relate to threats to safe navigation of merchant ships and fishing vessels. In addition there may be vessels involved in legal oil and mineral exploration at sea, in accordance with accepted international norms and laws. The threats faced are piracy, maritime terror, and disputes in APR erupting into open conflict, thus causing disruption of the global economy.

China has well known challenges in the APR. Its export oriented economy needs the sea for unhindered exports of goods, and also for energy imports. It is, therefore, building up its sea power to rival the US. Its primary aims are to regain control of Taiwan, establish its control over more than 200 islands in the SCS and ECS, breach the first two island chains, so as to control the Pacific ocean east of Hawaii, "resolve the Malacca dilemma" by controlling the SCS, and gain access to the IOR, with the eventual aim of controlling it, and becoming a genuine two ocean super power.

Rich APR nations like Japan, South Korea and Australia rely heavily on export for their economic growth, while they need energy imports. Australia is a major trading partner of China, and also a major US ally, she has allowed American marines a new base in Darwin. Other nations of the APR too need the sea for their economic growth. All APR nations along with others (including Singapore) are now enhancing their military capabilities to deal with China's coercive diplomacy in the region and are slowly becoming part of an undeclared alliance with USA.

The USA has declared a pivot Asia policy. It is establishing a 10 billion US dollar naval base in Guam, by 2020, while also increasing its naval presence in the APR to 60% of the total US Naval strength. This process will be completed by 2020, and till then the US has to face the challenge of China's new coercive diplomacy in APR, which began in 2012. The Chinese are aware of the military buildup in the APR and have decided to increase the pressure, before the other nations build up adequate military capabilities.

India has vital interests in the APR, and she has been re-invited by Vietnam in August 2012 to explore oil and gas in its waters in the SCS. India needs to expedite the buildup of its naval capabilities to ensure that it can protect its interests in the IOR and APR.

Session - II

Third Paper

Sr Col Le Kim Dung

Implications of Climate Change and Water Management on Regional Security

The Fourth Report of the United Nations Intergovernmental Panel on Climate Change states that Southeast Asia region suffers the most due to climate change. This region has to cope with many natural disasters such as storms, floods, and draught which has become more serious due to the rising of sea water level. Climate change has been making significant negative effects on regional agriculture, coastline system and the environment as well. It also creates a number of new regional security challenges.

The presentation will include the regional security challenges which are under the effects of climate change and water management, and convey some ideas on the Vietnam People's Army's experiences in order to cope with those security challenges.

The Regional Security Issues which Become More Serious due to Climate Change

Climate change is characterised by global warming,which melts the ice in the poles and as a result the sea water level rises and this has a significant effect on the Southeast Asia nations, since most of them (except Laos) are littoral countries. Vietnam ranks 23rd amongst the 193 nations listed in the Climate Change Vulnerability Index (CCVI), according to the Special Report on Managing the Risks of Extreme Events and Disasters to Advance Climate Change Adaptation (SREX). If sea level rises by one meter at the end of the 21 century then it is estimated that 40% of the total area of the Mekong Delta, 11% of the Red River delta and 3% of the coastal areas will be flooded. From 10% to 20% of the total population will be directly affected and losses can be up to 10% of the total GDP. The weather in the country has changed due to prolonged dry seasons, sudden floods, increasing saltwater intrusion, drought and landslides along the sea. By 2050, around 1 million people in the Mekong Delta will have to move due to climate change. Thailand has to suffer the same situation. It is important to indicate that the flooded areas are "the biggest rice baskets" of the countries, of the region as well as of the world. With the rice cultivating area reduced, the rising sea water level increases the saltwater intrusion, drought and floods become more rampant in the littoral countries. As a result, the crop productivity will suffer heavily, and food security will become the most challenging aspect of all countries in the region. It is not only making significant effects to this region but also spells disaster to the entire world.

However, the reduced production of crops is only one side of the coin. Climate change has also led to an increase in forest fires, diseases, environmental pollution, social crimes and poverty, thus resulting in increase of population migrating from villages to cities. This new immigration wave causes a greater number of social problems that we have to solve.

Many research projects have proved that the main reasons that create climate change are caused by human-beings such as glasshouse effects by manufactures, deforesting for timber etc. Due to rapid industrialization, the deforesting has not been controlled, immigrants have increased in the cities, leading to poverty and making this region vulnerable to the impact of climate change.

The fresh water resources have been exhausted because of rise in sea water level and increased consumption.. Climate change is linked closely with water management. As estimated by the UN, nearly a half of world population will face water problems by 2030 because of climate change. As population is rapidly increasing, Southeast Asia has more demand for food, water and energy. Water in Mekong, the biggest river in the region, has been exploited tremendously to fulfil the demands of argiculture and electricity. The Mekong and its tributaries provide food, water and transportation to about 60 million people in Cambodia, Laos, Thailand and Vietnam.

Role of the Vietnam People's Army (VPA) in Coping with Security Challenges emerging due to Climate Change

The VPA is one of the main forces of the country in coping with security issues including challenges by climate change. Fulfilling its basic function of combat readiness, sovereignty, unity, territorial integrity, and national interests, the VPA is well organized,. The Army helps in providing relief during floods, draughts, storms etc which have become more common and difficult to forecast in Vietnam. The VPA is also strengthening its ability to cope with social problems caused by climate change such as illegal migration, social crimes etc.The VPA supports and takes part in green economy that promotes greenhouse gas mitigation for sustainable development. Many VPA institutions are carrying out research projects on climate change. Functioning as an army ready for work, the VPA has always maintained close ties with the people. The VPA supports and takes part in international cooperation to achieve the common goal of climate change mitigation and sustainable development. Defence cooperation is one of the most important factors to cope with regional security and climate change. Therefore, Vietnam advocates expanding defence cooperation in the regional and international community for this end. The VPA advocates effectively broadening and increasing bilateral defence cooperation with neighbouring countries and other ASEAN countries, to solve regional security issues which are caused by climate change.

Session - II

Fourth Paper

Mr. Ivan Safranchuk

Energy, Environmental and Maritime Security

Since 19th Centaury, Russia has been active political player in Asia. Even more so after WW II, when Asian countries became prominent for world competition between two "grand camps" – Capitalism and Communism, headed by the US and the USSR respectively.

The USSR was deeply involved in Asian politics and provided huge volumes of economic assistance to its allies and partners in Asia. Besides for many Asian countries with aspirations for progress and industrial development, the USSR was the primary source of technology and equipment. The Soviet Union went through unprecedented industrialization programme in the decades of 1930-1940. For progressive countries in the world the Soviet Union was the model of high speed economic and industrial projects. The USSR was willing to share its experience with Asian states, by providing technology, equipment and education. However; two factors were relevant in the second half of the 20th Century in Asia.

First, Asia was the battle field in the Cold War. Consequently, Asian countries were receiving assistance from outside the region. Nobody viewed Asia as the centre of gravity of world economics.

Second, in Asia bipolarity was diffused while the US and the USSR tended to see the world and regions from bipolar perspective. With India and China keeping "special position" in the Cold War, Asia was multipolar.

After the collapse of the USSR in 1991, Asia moved to periphery of Russian decision-makers. Russia needed assistance and investment opportunities as it was undergoing economic and social turmoil. In the 1990s Western countries were the only source of both. Consequently, Russian policy became West-oriented. This was underpinned also by ideological factor. President Boris Yeltsin put his political stake on the reformers, who wanted to westernize Russia up to the point of becoming part of the West, dreaming about equal and true partnership with the US and European countries.

Russia turned to Asia politically, only after she faced painful disappointment in relations with the West. Like in 1993, when contrary to earlier promises, NATO expansion was set on track. Or like in 1999, when NATO invaded Serbia or in 2003, when the US invaded Iraq. In most political cases (NATO expansion, Missile Defense, etc) Russia found common ground with China.

Russian political interest in Asia increased but economically Russia was focused on the West. Russia made note of the growing Asian economies. However; deep crisis of "Asian tigers" in 1997-1998 was interpreted like the continuing Western predominance in world economy.

The two links kept Russian interest in Asia. These were the trade relations with India and China. Massive arms contracts, which are never free of politics, kept not only relatively high volumes of trade, but also high political interest.

In the mid 2000s, Russian industries sensed the shift of demand for raw materials and commodities from Asia and became eager to develop new export opportunities in Asia. Russia's financial and industrial tycoons, who in the previous years had been implementing aggressive expansion strategies mostly through mergers ended up in debt due to 2008 economic meltdown. They started looking for options in the Asia financial markets.

Russia saw Asia as the new centre of gravity for world economy. True partnership with the West did not materialize. Contrary to earlier expectations, Russia got interested in becoming a real stake-holder in Asian economic boom.

Russia has the potential to contribute to the Asian economic growth in four areas: 1) Supply of energy and commodities. 2) Transportation and transit. 3) Food supply. 4) Arms and high technology weapon systems.

Russian Western Siberian resources are connected to the European market through the developed infrastructure. However; the development of

Eastern Siberian and Far Eastern resources can be connected to Europe and Asia. Russia wants to increase supply to growing Asian economies. What lacks is infrastructure. To improve infrastructure Russia wants to invest in new pipelines in Asian parts of the country.

At the moment 99 per cent of the trade between Asia and Europe goes through maritime transportation. However, modern technologies enable attractive option of railway transit through Russia. With modernization of railway system and improvement of administrative and customs procedures; transportation of containers can be twice quicker in time and comparable in price. This means further economy on insurance services due to less time of transportation and smaller railway risks and credit as the capital is less frozen in goods and quick availability for sale. Russian private sector with state support is working to resolve the problems. But still Russia will have only 5 per cent of total trade flow between Asia and Europe.

Food security is a major issue in Asia. Growth of population plus growing standards means increase in consumption. Russia became in the last decade an important grain-exporter. For developing its potential, Russia needs better access to Asian markets, by developing better infrastructure in the Russian Far East.

For export of high technology, arms and weapon systems, Russia is a traditional partner for big Asian countries.

The main problem Russia faces is the underdevelopment of infrastructure in its Asian parts, including seashore territories. Consequently Russia exploits economic opportunities in Asia by cooperating, with countries with which it has land borders. Practically this means China. China is the biggest Russian trade and economic partner in Asia. Political relations between the two countries are also cordial.

However, Asia for Russia is more than China. Russia wants to develop infrastructure, which will give better access to Asian seas and more countries in Asia. Better access to Asia-Pacific-Region will intensify economic relations with many countries of the region. This does not mean that Russia-China relations will deteriorate. Russia will just go beyond China, in Asia.

The driver of renewed Russian interest in Asia-Pacific-Region is economy. Russia wants to be a true stake-holder in Asian economic development. However; as Russia goes to Asia for economic opportunities; it faces more complicated political and security risks. Asia lacks institutions and mechanisms to endure peace and security. In Europe despite the war in the Balkans, and collapse of CFE treaty; security mechanism and institutions are more robust than in Asia.

The European experience reveals that nations go to war despite economic interdependence. Security is essential for continued economic growth in Asia. Russia with its economic interest in Asia will also contribute to regional security for peace in Asia and the Pacific.

Session II: Discussion

Issue Raised

In the wake of terror threats, there is concern about the safety of transportation of energy resources from Russia to Europe.

Response

Much of the energy resources are exported through pipelines. As LNG exports have increased, pipelines have been constructed which are economically more viable than containers. But when we look from security perspective, pipelines are not safe as these can be attacked easily. This is a big security threat.

Issue Raised

With the climate changing, ice is melting at the Arctic Ocean. This has opened avenues to access the unexplored energy resources. Russia is the frontline state in the context of Arctic region and has good accessibility. Would Russia transfer energy resources from the Arctic Ocean to Asian countries?

Response

Arctic exploration is a long term and costly project. For this the support of multi-national companies like BP are required. These companies will aim for Asian markets. Oil companies make money from Upstream and Downstream processes. Companies like BP donor have downstream infrastructure in the Asian Countries. This can make them divert the resources to Europe where they are well equipped and can make more profits. Asian countries should allow global MNCs to have downstream infrastructure in their countries.

Issue Raised

Central Asia has vast energy resources. Is there any possibility of transfer of these energy resources from Central Asia to India?

Response

For movement of energy resources from Central Asia to India proper infrastructure is required. The project like TAPI has complex security constraints.

Issue Raised

If there is any problem in South East Asia, then there is ASEAN to deal with it. If ASEAN fails to resolve it, the countries can ask the UN to mediate. In such a scenario, what is the role of the EU in Asia Pacific?

Response

It is difficult to form Multi-lateral organizations in Asia-Pacific. There are big powers like China and Russia and many middle powers are emerging. If EU has to play a role in Asia-Pacific, then it has to offer its experience and engage with countries politically. If they have to play a role in economics then there are opportunities. But EU can play a major role mostly through political frameworks.

Issue Raised

It is proposed to have institutionalization of relations between European region and Asia. What are your views on such a proposal?.

Response

It would be an integration process which perforce has to be mainly economic in nature. The details would need to be worked out and is bound to take considerable time.

Issue Raised

With the dwindling population in the far-east Russia, is there a chance of Chinese invasion in that area?

Response

There are some demographic problems in Russia's far-east, but it is not alarming. Russia does not see this as a security threat.

Session II

Chairman's Concluding Remarks

Vice Admiral PS Das, PVSM, AVSM, VSM (Retd)

The economic centre of gravity has shifted from Europe to the Asia-Pacific i.e. mainly from land to ocean. In Europe it was mainly military, but one cannot say that there will be wars in Asia-Pacific in the near future. At the same time Europe evolved into EU, it is not very easy for Asia to do so. In the Asia-Pacific, trend is to have bilateral arrangements. Bilateral arrangements should help in reducing tension between rivals. I would like to conclude this session with a remark that, today it is very essential for all states in the region to engage China, which has emerged as a big power. I would also like to thank the entire panel for sharing their views about Energy, Environment and Maritime Security in the Asia-PacificRegion.

SESSION - III

PANEL- 1

FUTURE SECURITY CHALLENGES AND OPPORTUNITIES

Chairman	Major General Dato' Pahlawan Dr. William R. Stevenson.
First Paper	Prof. Richard Rigby and Dr. Brendan Taylor.
Second Paper	Prof Swaran Singh.
Third Paper	Sr Col (Ms) Do Mai Khanh.
Fourth Paper	Dr. Satoru Nagao.

PANEL-2

Chairman	Air Chief Marshal SP Tyagi, PVSM, AVSM, VM (Retd).
First Paper	Dr. Daesung Song.
Second Paper	Dr. Elichi Kathara.
Third Paper	Major General BK Sharma, SM** (Retd).
Fourth Paper	Dr. Tuan Yao Cheng.
Discussion	
Concluding Remarks	

Session -III
Panel -1
Chairperson
Major General Dato' Pahlawan Dr William R. Stevenson

Today's topic is "Future Security Challenges and Opportunities" in the Asia-Pacific. The rise of powers in international arena has led to complex security challenges. To talk about this issue we have five distinguished scholars. The first paper will be presented jointly by Prof Richard Rigby and Dr. Brendon Taylor, both from Australian National University (ANU), Australia. Prof. Swaran Singh who is a Professor in Jawaharlal Nehru University (JNU), India will be the next. The third paper will be by Sr. Col (Ms.) Do Mai Khanh from IDIR, Vietnam and finally by Dr Satoru Nagao from OPRF, Japan.

I welcome Prof Richard Rigby to present the paper to be followed by Dr. Brendon Taylor.

Session-III

Panel-1

First Paper

Prof. Richard Rigby and Dr. Brendan Taylor

The Indo-Pacific As a Strategic System: An Australian Perspective

The Indo-Pacific has become something of a catchphrase in Australian strategic policy circles. Defence Minister Stephen Smith, a prominent advocate of the term, has recently observed that the Indo-Pacific 'will become the world's strategic centre of gravity.' In similar vein, current Australian High Commissioner to India and recently announced Secretary of the Australian Department of Foreign Affairs and Trade (DFAT), Peter Varghese, has suggested that 'today, it makes more sense to think of the Indo-Pacific, rather than the Asia Pacific, as the crucible of Australian security.'

Australian academics and think tanks have also embraced the term. In his award winning book, former director of the Lowy Institute for International Policy, Michael Wesley, refers to an 'Indo-Pacific power highway [that] takes the pivot of world power away from the northern Pacific and northern Atlantic and shifts it to the southern and eastern coasts of the Asian landmass.' Rory Medcalf, also of the Lowy Institute, argues that the 'Indo-Pacific is a viable definition of the broad region of principal strategic and economic importance to Australia, now and in all likelihood well into this century.' Academics Nick Bisley and Andrew Phillips go even further, asserting that the Indo-pacific is a key guiding strategic principle that has 'arrived.'

Attraction for Australia

At least four factors can be seen to account for this burgeoning interest in the Indo-Pacific as a strategic construct. First and foremost, the Indo-Pacific appeals to Australian policy elites because it alleviates a longstanding apprehension of political and economic exclusion from Asia. The late Harvard Political Scientist, Samuel Huntington, famously referred to Australia as a 'torn country' that has traditionally faced an uphill battle in its efforts to engage with the Asian region due, in part, to its 'otherness' in the eyes of Asian elites. In his terms, 'they have made it clear that if Australia wants to be part of Asia it must become truly Asian, which they think unlikely if not impossible.' Australian fears of economic exclusion from Asia were heightened in the early 1990s with the introduction of Malaysian Prime Minister Mahathir's 'East Asian Economic Caucus' proposal. It resurfaced momentarily in the early 2000s, as 'East Asian Community' sentiment grew in popularity, until Australia's 2005 admission to the East Asia Summit alleviated these concerns somewhat. From Canberra's perspective, one of the benefits of the Indo-Pacific construct is that it essentially puts to bed these enduring questions of whether or not Australia is part of Asia.

Second, and just as significantly, Australian attraction to the Indo-Pacific construct relates to the fact that it is consistent with America's Asia strategy. At present, its usage thus serving as a useful vehicle through which to demonstrate alliance solidarity. In recent years a sharp public debate has been played out in Australia as to whether Canberra will ultimately be forced to make a choice between its leading trading partner (China) and its longstanding strategic ally (the United States). While serving and former politicians – including former Prime Minister Paul Keating – have weighed in on this debate suggesting that Australia will indeed be forced to make such a choice, that view appears to have gained little traction thus far in Australian policy circles. Speaking to the US Congress in March 2011, Prime Minister Julia Gillard pledged that 'Australia is an ally for all the years to come.' Reinforcing such sentiment, the Indo-Pacific construct is consistent with a number of more practical - albeit still rather symbolic – commitments that the Australian government has made in support of the US alliance over the past 12 months, including an agreement to rotate up to 2,500 marines annually through facilities in Northern Australia. The prospect of increased American Navy access to *HMAS Sterling*, which Defence Minister Smith describes as 'Australia's Indian Ocean port', is likewise supportive of these trends.

Australian enthusiasm for the Indo-Pacific concept also stems from a desire to deepen strategic ties with India. For decades, security relations between Canberra and New Delhi have remained severely underdeveloped, dogged by issues relating to Australia's alliance with the US – India's nuclear weapons programme and, more recently, attacks on Indian nationals studying in Australia. As Wesley has noted, however, for the first time in recent history some convergence in Australia's and India's 'strategic imaginations' is emerging. This convergence is in part driven by mutual concerns regarding how rising China might use its growing power. For Australia, the Indian Ocean region has taken on a renewed significance in this context. Australia's region has also taken on renewed strategic significance for New Delhi as it strives to deepen ties with Southeast Asian countries as part of its 'Look East' policy. The November 2009 Australia-India Security declaration, coupled with the Labor Party's more recent decision to support the sale of Uranium to India, both reflect and serve to further facilitate this convergence in strategic mind-set. To be sure, it is a convergence that will not be without difficulties and limits. From Canberra's perspective, however, the Indo-Pacific serves as a useful framework within which to strive to progress.

Last, but certainly not least, the Indo-Pacific construct is also consistent with a concomitant Australian desire to deepen its strategic relationship with Indonesia. Australia's relationship with Indonesia has also historically been a troubled one, with Canberra caught between viewing Indonesia as a strategic asset and a strategic liability. The last decade in Australia-Indonesia relations has been something of a 'golden period', however, with cooperation between the Australian and Indonesian police forces forged out of the ashes of the October 2002 Bali Bombings – in which 88 Australian national were killed – serving as a catalyst for deeper security ties. This deepening in relations was reflected with the inauguration in March 2012 of a new two-plus-two dialogue between the foreign and defence ministers of Australia and Indonesia. Once again, this relationship is also not without its tensions, including most recently over the Australian banning of live cattle exports to Indonesia. However, as Indonesia's growth continues to the point where respectable projections see it joining the ranks of the world's top five economies by the year 2030, strategic policymakers are eager to shape a positive relationship with this rising power which, all going well, could potentially even offer Australia a degree of shelter from the great power machinations unfolding further North. Because Indonesia's strategic geography - which also straddles the Indian and Pacific Oceans – renders it an Indo-Pacific power in every sense of the term, Australia's use of this nomenclature thus needs to be viewed in this context.

Costs for Canberra

The Indo-Pacific construct is not without its detractors. One criticism that can be levelled at Canberra's embrace of the term is that it is unduly provocative to Beijing. The Australia-China relationship has certainly been a testy one in recent times. Going back to 2009 – a year when former Australian Ambassador to China Geoff Raby, recently characterized as an 'annus horribilis' for the bilateral relationship – rifts have opened up over a raft of issues including references to China in the Australian Defence White Paper of 2009 and the decision of the Australian government during the same year to grant a visa to Uyghur human rights advocate, Rebiya Kadeer, allowing her to attend the Melbourne International Film festival. More recently, US President Barack Obama's November 2011 announcement that up to 2,500 marines would be deployed to Darwin has reportedly generated further tensions in the relationship. While this latest development is arguably of marginal genuine strategic significance, for Beijing it is the thinking behind this initiative and the perception that it is part of a larger US-led strategy to 'contain' China's rising power that is most objectionable. Because the Indo-Pacific construct aligns with America's current rebalancing strategy, a case can be made that Canberra's enthusiasm for the terminology will act as a further irritant in the Australia-China bilateral relationship.

Second, and relatedly, other Australian critics of the Indo-Pacific construct argue that, by explicitly seeking to amplify Australia's strategic significance to the US, advocates of the term will significantly increase the costs of the American alliance to Canberra. Bisley and Phillips – two leading exponents of this line of thinking – argue their case in the following terms:

By making Australia more important to the United States, Canberra invites understandable expectations from Washington that it will do more, pay for more and assume a far more visible role in propping up American primacy, particularly in the Indian Ocean region. Leading-edge indicators of what additional commitments to a more Indo-Pacific-oriented ANZUS might entail include on-going discussions about increased US naval access to HMAS Sterling, as well as proposals to station a US drone base in the Coco Islands. Considered in isolation, such proposals are unlikely to invite concern. But seen through the lens of a United States increasingly keen to share the burden of maintaining regional order with 'deputy sheriffs' old and new, they potentially foreshadow a more demanding and obtrusive alliance.

A number of other respected analysts of Australian strategic policy have joined Bisley and Phillips in expressing similar caution, arguing that while their country has made politically and symbolically significant contributions to the American alliance over the sixty-plus years of its existence, Canberra has cleverly been able to achieve what amounts to a 'free ride' in this relationship – as reflected in the disproportionately small military contributions Australia has made to major operations in Korea, Vietnam, Afghanistan and Iraq. Invoking the Indo-Pacific construct, in their view, threatens to unnecessarily and unwisely break with a highly pragmatic and largely effective – if somewhat morally suspect – approach that Australia has thus far managed to get away with.

A third downside to employing the term is the sense of incoherence it creates in Australian foreign and security policy. Within the past half-decade alone, Australian policymakers have used a number of descriptors to characterize the Asian region. During his truncated time in office, for instance, Prime Minister Kevin Rudd famously referred to an 'Asia-Pacific' region, as epitomized by his ill-fated Asia-Pacific community proposal of June 2008. Partly in an effort to assert her foreign policy credentials at a time when Rudd's subsequent activism as Foreign Minister was generating heightened speculation of his possible return to the Prime Ministership, Prime Minister Gillard in September 2011 commissioned an 'Asian Century' White Paper. His move to the backbench notwithstanding, Rudd has continued to employ the Asia-Pacific nomenclature in a number of high profile speeches pointing out the need for a new 'Pax Pacifica' that will enable the region to accommodate China's rise. To be sure, a common thread running through these various descriptors is that they each include Australia as part of the region which, as Huntington's aforementioned analysis highlights, has not always been assumed by Asian policy elites. That said the terms 'Asia', 'Asia-Pacific', 'Pacific' and 'Indo-Pacific' are clearly not synonymous. Hence, their concurrent usage by Australian policymakers is potentially confusing.

Finally, the term Indo-Pacific is problematic in that it remains ill-defined. Defence Minister Smith, for instance, has referred to the construct as an amalgam of 'the Asia-Pacific and the Indian Ocean Rim.' Varghese, by contrast, seems to adopt a much narrower formulation when he describes the Indo-Pacific construct as matching 'neatly' with the recently expanded East Asia Summit (EAS), in line with Wesley who sees that organization as providing 'an institutional recognition of an Indo-Pacific dynamic'. Whether the Indo-Pacific presently constitutes, or is ever likely to constitute, a 'strategic system' in any genuine sense is also open to question. As Medcalf, one of the leading Australian advocates of the construct was recently forced to concede, 'certainly there will be some important security dynamics that remain principally concentrated in one or other of these sub regions, such as Korean Peninsula tensions in North Asia or India-Pakistan relations on the subcontinent.' Along with the 'Taiwan problem' – which falls into a similar category – the fact that these flashpoints are arguably Asia's most dangerous suggests that this particular deficiency with the Indo-Pacific construct cannot be too readily dismissed.

Where to go from here?

These criticisms and shortcomings notwithstanding, Defence Minister Smith's public pronouncements on the subject strongly suggest that the Indo-Pacific construct will be given prominence in the forthcoming 2013 Australian Defence White Paper. This is not altogether surprising. Australia's foreign and strategic policy tradition has traditionally been one of pragmatic realism. For the near term at least, Canberra will likely continue its use of the term as a device for avoiding marginalization from the region, supporting continued US engagement in this part of the world, and deepening its strategic engagement with India and Indonesia.

Looking to the longer term, Australia's continued attraction to the Indo-Pacific construct remains contingent upon how strategic relations between Asia's great powers unfold. Should we be entering a period of deepening strategic competition between these powers – a scenario many Australian analysts see as likely - the term may well catch on? A number of American and Indian analysts have certainly shown interest in utilizing the term, more so in the context of responding to China's rise than has perhaps been the case for Australia. It is not inconceivable that the term could exhibit similar appeal for Tokyo also as it seeks to further deepen its ties with the US and India in the face of China's rise. Somewhat ironically, however, notwithstanding the fact that China - much like Australia and Indonesia – is arguably an Indo-Pacific power in the classic sense, such dynamics will almost certainly continue to lessen its appeal to Beijing.

By the same token, an Indo-Pacific strategic system that does not include China would be a contradiction in terms. Accordingly, if we wish to bring the construct closer to fruition, it will be important to find ways of engaging China's interest in a positive fashion, to avoid the appearance of seeking in some way to contain China – a weakness, notwithstanding denials, of the original 'Quad' concept. One way to do this would be through the EAS, in line with the arguments of both Varghese and Wesley. Given China's growing interests in the Indian Ocean region – reliance on Middle East oil, importance of safe sea-lines of communication, the 'Malacca Straits dilemma' and so on, the idea of an Indo-Pacific system should, logically, have greater resonance with China than it may once have done.

Session -III
Panel-1
Second Paper

Prof Swaran Singh

Deconstructing Future Security Trends

The power and paradigm shift of global politics from Euro-Atlantic to Asia-Pacific has been gradually unfolding. Its contours, the pace of drift remains slow and direction less defined than expected. For the discernible signposts, the United States continues to be the leader even in the Asia-Pacific theatre and meanwhile a whole range of non-state actors have become important stakeholders especially in view of nations preferring to leverage their economic and cultural instruments of soft-power paradigm. The hard-power, their armed forces however; continue to underwrite fundamental trends and outcomes. So it is in their potential projections, and not actual reality, that major Asia-Pacific countries – especially civilizational states like China and India – see the promise of becoming the centre of gravity in 21st century world affairs.

In terms of its credentials, the Asia-Pacific-Region today counts for over one-third of global population, nearly one-third of global exports and about two-thirds of total global foreign exchange reserves. This means that bulk of manufacturing and purchasing power has shifted towards this region. Increasingly, their large populations are no longer seen as a liability. Moreover, the recent global economic slowdown in the industrialized world since 2007 has further accelerated power-shift from Atlantic to the Pacific, from hard to soft power. China is now the largest trading partner for most countries and this is making the US and its allies increasingly worried. China's expanding footprint accompanied by rapid military modernization has unleashed debates about post-American world.

Asia-Pacific continues to be engulfed in conventional issues of conflict and is getting increasingly exposed to a whole range of non-conventional threats and challenges. This region has states that have nuclear weapons but are not yet so recognized as part of nuclear order of the nuclear non-proliferation treaty (NPT). These include countries like Israel, India, Pakistan, and North Korea who have weapons and yet are not so recognized by major powers. Then there are conflicts about Korean peninsula, Taiwan, South China Sea and several other territorial disputes that continue to undermine regional peace and stability as nations get bogged down by additional threats from piracy, resource-scarcity, climate change and energy security. As they begin to get a grip on these non-traditional threats to security, their conventional disputes continue to complicate the regional environment.

It is in this backdrop that this dynamic region has demonstrated strong and continued commitment for professing and practicing ASEAN-led multilateralism which has attracted major powers participation. Only the progress remains extremely slow in achieving its targets. This is so because this brand remains vulnerable to its fundamental weakness of never hurting critical interest of major powers who see themselves as stakeholders in the Asia-Pacific. Moreover, these ASEAN-led experiments in multilateralism across the Asia-Pacific have begun to witness power struggles between China and US and its allies.

The Big Picture is changing

With time and space crunch phenomenon affecting all aspects of universe, the exponential pace of change in human life is also transforming the nature of international power politics. As regards the short and medium term future of the Asia-Pacific-Region from this perspective, noticeable trends of change are summarized in succeeding paragraphs.

First, the US is and will, most likely, remain the preponderant power with its continued military presence across the region. Therefore, in near and medium term US will continue to define the agenda for security in the Asia-Pacific-Region. Even metaphors like 'power' and 'security' will also be getting increasingly broad based and complicated. What constitutes security threats and how to tackle these will be determined by the US, though US mind set will be increasingly influenced by its interface with the countries of Asia-Pacific or by their diaspora inside these countries. Whites in US will soon become a minority creating space for other ethnic communities.

Second, despite overwhelming disparity between US military 'power' compared with any other nation or combination of nations across Asia-Pacific, US ability to influence outcomes will continue to diminish relatively. The pace of diminishing influence could be accelerated by events like global economic slowdown or drifts in internal politics of major powers which may be caused by their demographic changes as also their increasing connectivity with the rest of humanity. Climate change debates have revealed how post-Industrial Revolution life style can be sustained only at its own peril, which presents a very different trigger for 'global' initiatives. In coming years, major powers will have to learn to understand and internalize such drifts and respond with innovative strategies that will underwrite the nature of their evolving relation with the rest of the Asia-Pacific nations.

Third, the larger trend of globalization will continue to erode the power of State and make non-State and extra-regional actors and agencies far more influential in local decision-making. State sovereignty is no longer viewed as power but responsibility and state will become increasingly vulnerable to the scrutiny by external and internal watch-dogs. While success of governments will lay in forging new partnerships they will have to make space for new stakeholders instead of imposing their writ. There is also going to be increasing demand for transparency and accountability, as also increasing wave in favour of liberal democracy and public-private partnerships. This will have impact on international and regional politics, making it more nuanced.

Fourth, China's rise and its implications for the Asia-Pacific remain daunting given the wide gap in perceptions about its security strategies and trajectories of growth. This is the first time since Greco-Roman times that a civilizational state has the power to unleash systemic changes if not to altogether rewrite the regional or global order. But starting from early 1990s, China-threat theories of western world have cast China into an evil mould worldwide and this seems a difficult gulf to bridge. China no doubt remains intriguing case study especially when viewed from Anglo-Saxon lenses. But without a common or mutual understanding to develop joint strategies amongst Asia-Pacific countries, this power and paradigm shift can prove counterproductive and fuel intra-regional dissensions.

Finally, while military conflicts between states are less likely to occur, their joint multilateral arrangements to deal with their old and new threats will remain nascent and inflexible and, therefore, wield limited influence and efficacy. Their conventional arrangements remain state-centric and fail to accommodate new stakeholders and address new systemic pressure-points. Architectures of security cooperation have to be adjusted accordingly and made increasingly locally grounded. Besides, Asia-Pacific remains so diverse with varying perceptions and priorities that it will not be possible to develop a common pan-Asia-Pacific understanding on its future trajectories leave aside finding answers to tackle security threats that flow from there.

Changing Nature of Conflict

Prima facie, over 90 per cent of all wars today occur not between, but within states. Over 85 per cent of deaths in such wars are those of innocent civilians. It is the use of small arms and light weapons that has become most potent and largest killer. Therefore, security now involves protecting and providing for communities within a country rather than defending its territorial boundaries against external enemies. Most violence today is unleashed by irregular forces and on unarmed civilians in order to intimidate and engage in ethnic cleansing. Terrorism has come to be their favoured tactics with no respect for any legal or moral restraints. This seems to be the emerging picture of the nature of conflict.

Asia-Pacific-Region will continue to be vulnerable to changing nature of conflict as it remains exposed to several conventional threats as well non-conventional threats that together will accentuate intra-state situations and, therefore, inter-State equations. For instance, China considers Taiwan its reneged province and Korean peninsula remains most militarized border, with both sides arming themselves with dangerous weapons. One could add Afghanistan, Pakistan, India, Indonesia, the Philippines, Thailand and even Arab Spring to influence trends in Asia-Pacific-Region. Rising tensions in China's equations with Japan and several other maritime neighbours around South China Sea will continue to carry the potential to create regional instability. And, increasingly, US new initiatives – like Trans-Pacific Partnership or Indo-Pacific formulations and deployments – continue to ignore if not counter China which seems to be the major trigger for these new initiatives from both sides of this expanding divide across theAsia-Pacific-Region.

Multilateralism is the Key

Given the diversity of Asia-Pacific countries, communitarian kind of multilateralism will remain the key to ensuring stability and peace in this region. While the multilateral structures of Cold War years like the South East Asian Treaty Organization (SEATO) or Central Treaty Organization (CENTO) have been consigned into history, ASEAN-led community building project remains very fragile and piecemeal to lend any wider confidence as yet. Moreover, even within existing ASEAN-led multilateral forums there remain visible power struggle especially between China on the one side and the US and its allies on the other. Given this reality, ASEAN-led initiatives remain restrained in not doing anything that may potentially hurt interests of any of the major powers which makes these ineffective though ASEAN has so far managed to stay in driver's seat in Asia-Pacific multilateral forums.

Deeper than that, the process of regionalization and regional identity though relatively strong at the level of various sub-regions remain elusive at the level of Asia-Pacific-Region. This has to do with extreme diversity of nature of terrain (continental, archipelagic, landlocked, long-coasts), size, level of development, nature of politics, religion and culture. Varying outlooks flowing from Islam, Buddhism, Hinduism, and Christianity are further complicated by nature of political regimes. As a result, in spite of great discomfiture amongst most Asia-Pacific countries, it is the US hub-and-spokes that continue to articulate and underwrite the regional peace and security order. So other than gradual and piecemeal rise of ASEAN-led multilateralism, Asia-Pacific security will remain dependent on the resident preponderant power – the United Sates – reorganizing its partnerships with conventional allies from Japan, South Korea to Australia and New Zealand and forging new partnerships across Asia-Pacific-Region.

The longer-term trends in international politics though will favour ASEAN-led communitarian multilateralism as that will become the way of conducting international relations. Given the spectre of globalization and connectedness of nations, all security and development needs of every nation would require working with several other nations. In this post-Westphalia world, the post-American world may not be devoid of US leadership and may only mean greater coordination amongst nations. But this will sure open new opportunities for expanded role of Asia-Pacific countries in determining both their own futures as also future of the whole world. But these long-term projections may slow down or even derail given possibilities of hiccups like 9/11 and economic slowdown which have brought focus back on elements of hard power and eroding value of norms and institutions that can accommodate extreme diversities of Asia-Pacific-Region.

Conclusion

In terms of mid-term future projections for Asia-Pacific-Region, there remain strong possibilities of current trends of power and paradigm shift causing a systemic transformation. But while discourses on soft-power, diffusion of power, comprehensive power will continue to propagate common, cooperative, collective brands of frameworks for regional security, trends of peace and security in Asia-Pacific will continue to be determined by hard power. And here, recent 25 years may have witnessed a phenomenal increase in defence expenditures of the Asia-Pacific nations – especially China moving from $15 billion in 1988 to $125 billion for 2011 (in constant 2010 dollars value) – this remains far less compared to US defence expenditure hovering around $700 billion making US the paramount power.

More recent trends of economic slowdown for last five years and Eurozone crisis may have triggered speculations of Asia-Pacific led by China, is catching up with the developed world led by US, faster than existing projections, but it also carries potential of US and China falling in trap of divisive impulses thereby creating additional structural stress for regional order. Alternative scenario could involve China taking the lead in building an economic order while US taking a lead in building a security order for Asia-Pacific-Region. But even this will not be without its frictions given their mutual suspicions. China's economic rise has clearly been accompanied by rapid military modernisation. Its continued generous responses to world's economic crisis are, therefore, viewed in the context of its burgeoning military modernization programme and growing role in the integration initiatives across Asia-Pacific-Region. Most of the challenges for Asia-Pacific peace and security in coming decades, therefore, will flow from how the US and China manage their equations.

Session-III

Panel-1

Third Paper

Sr Col (Ms) Do Mai Khanh

Future Security Challenges and Opportunities

Asia Pacific is one of the most important regions in terms of geopolitics and geo-economy, which comprises vital sea lanes of communication, linking Pacific to Indian Ocean. Asia Pacific embeds almost world powers, makes up half of the world's population and is rich in natural resources. It has become the most dynamic region of the world with emerging economies and growing linkage and integration. It attracts ever- increasing attention from other extra-regional countries.

However, in the context of current geopolitics change and shift, regional security issues are emerging as challenges to sustainable peace and stability. The increasing engagement by major powers into the region also means increase in potential clashes of interest among them. Such a security environment requires more responsibility and efforts by regional countries to ensure peace, stability and development.

Most of the history of the 21st century will be written in Asia and Asia Pacific will bear both security challenges and opportunities.

Future Security Challenges

Power competition

Major Powers' engagement in the region, on one hand creates more opportunities for promoting regional cooperation and integration, and on the other hand, would turn the region into area of their potential influence. In this context, the Sino-US relation continues to be seen as the most important element in shaping regional security architecture and influencing other relations. Although, facing difficulties in its economic development and consequent relative decline of its strength, the US is still the superpower of the world. In the past decades, China has grown at a faster pace, thus challenging the US's status. China is now the US's biggest rival in the world, especially in the Asia Pacific region. The US-Sino relation embraces the intertwined cooperative and competitive factors. In a globalised world, the US and China are more interdependent, especially in economic terms. Besides, one needs the other's support and cooperation in regional and international issues.

Competition and clashes of interest among major powers affect the region as well as regional countries which might be drawn into competition.

Territorial and Maritime Disputes

There exist many territorial disputes in almost every part of Asia Pacific. Given the growing importance of the sea, maritime disputes over islands and waters will continue to be complicated, threatening the peace and stability of the region. Many countries depend on seas for their development. They go to seas, exploring and exploiting natural resources for their development. They also project their power and capabilities in seas to expand their space of controls and influence, protect their interest at sea and guarantee safe vital sea lanes of communication for transportation. These actions would result in more disputes and clashes at sea. In addition, the growing nationalism, instability and domestic politics of some regional countries would increase the danger of tension and conflicts concerning the disputes. The region will need more effective mechanisms which could facilitate the settlement of disputes and prevent possible conflicts.

Arms Race

Arms race is seen as a potential threat to the security of the region. In recent years, regional countries have increased their defence budgets. They spent more on the acquisition of military weapons and equipment. It is reported in Military Balance 2012 that the total defence expenses of Asian countries in 2011 had an increase of 3.15%. And according to the International Institute for Strategic Studies (IISS), in 2012, Asia's defence expenditure has surpassed that of the Europeans for the first time.

The economic growth has facilitated and supported the expenditure of regional countries in the past years. The purpose of increased defence spending varies from country to country. Besides, unsettled disputes, unstable security flash-points and lack of confidence and trust would contribute to the rising defence expenditure. An arms race if it is not managed and controlled can increase danger of conflicts.

Flash-points of the Cold War

The flash-points from the Cold War era including Korean Peninsula and Taiwan Straits, continue to be potential security challenges in the region as they relate to interests of major powers. The lack of mutual confidence and trust mechanism could adversely affect regional security.

Non-traditional Security Issues

Terrorism is a threat to the security of the region. Regional governments have adopted certain measures to prevent terrorism. However, danger of bomb attacks in some regional countries still continues.

Transnational crimes, natural disasters, pandemics, climate change and so on continue to adversely affect the security environment of the region. These challenges can have severe consequences. In addition, food, energy, sources of water, and environmental issues are also emerging as major challenges, especially in the developing and under-developed countries.

Future Security Opportunities

Cooperation for economic development and growing integration have led to interdependence among countries. Regional countries share interest in ensuring an environment of peace and stability for development. Although, there are unsettled disputes in the region, possibility of a large-scale conflict in the region is remote. Conflicts will not solve problems and, therefore, these will not be the choice of the countries for resolving disputes. The desire for peace and stable environment hopefully will bring the countries together for dialogue and discussions for settling security issues.

Treaty of Amity and Cooperation (TAC) and Southeast Asia Nuclear Weapon Free Zone (SEANWFZ) established and developed by the ASEAN have been supported by countries. ASEAN and China also signed the Declaration on the Code of Conduct of Parties in South China Sea (DOC) and are working to achieve the Code of Conduct (COC). It is expected to prevent conflicts in the South China Sea.

Regional security architecture is being renewed to meet requirements of the changing security environment. Various cooperative mechanisms have been established in recent years. ASEAN+1, ASEAN+3, APEC, EAS, ARF, ADMM/ADMM+, Shangri-La Dialogue have become important. These have helped in building confidence, trust and sharing experience. The aim is to ensure peace and stability and build a secure environment.

Conclusion

Asia Pacific is one of the most important regions. Although regional linkages and integration are on the rise; peace, cooperation, stability and development remain the main agenda. The region is facing traditional and non-traditional security issues. In the context of the changing world, Asia Pacific is facing both security challenges and opportunities. Therefore, regional countries should make use of the opportunities to promote dialogue and cooperation, manage the disputes and prevent conflicts thereby ensuring peace and stability in this region.

Session-III

Panel-1

Fourth Paper

Dr. Satoru Nagao

Why Japan Needs India as Security Provider?

When we think about Japan-India military relations as they stand today, we cannot forget one fact that Japan is located far from India. For example, from Tokyo, Japanese must spend ten hours to visit New Delhi by air. However, if we want to visit Los Angeles in USA, we spend same ten hours by air. The database of Ministry of Foreign Affairs in Japan points out that about 5,500 Japanese lived in India in 2011 but about 400,000 Japanese lived in USA. 140,000 Japanese lived in China and 12,000 Japanese lived in Indonesia. Compared with these numbers, there are relatively fewer Japanese in India. Geographical distance between Japan and India has been the primary reason for fewer military relations between the two countries historically.

However, nowadays, further cooperation in military relations between Japan and India is more and more plausible. Japan and India have already started a 2 + 2 dialogue (secretary level) and an annual exercise called Japan-India Maritime Exercise (JIMEX). It was the first time in 2012 that Japan participated in the Indian Ocean Naval Symposium (IONS). It is important to bear in mind that Japan has not entered into such kind of a deep security relationship with other countries except US and Australia. This makes the military ties between Japan and India a very important exceptional case.

Therefore, this paper will seek to analyze the context in which Japan-India military relations are gaining importance in Asia. From the viewpoint of the current power game in Asia, there are three important factors to this analysis i.e. US, ASEAN, and Japan.

US Needs Japan-India Cooperation

Firstly, US need an "ally" to maintain military balance in Asia because their naval power is declining and China's naval power is rising.

After the Cold War, US lost the reason to maintain large number of warships in their navy. In 1990, US Navy possessed 15 aircraft carriers, 230 "big surface combatants" which were more than 3000t of full load displacement and 127 submarines which included 126 nuclear submarines. However; by 2012, US Navy consisted only of 11 aircraft carriers, 110 "big surface combatants" and 72 nuclear submarines. And by next year, US will reduce one aircraft carrier and nine "big surface combatants" and add one nuclear submarine. Despite what the US Secretary of Defence Leon Panetta said at the annual Shangri-La Dialogue, "By 2020, the Navy will re posture its forces, from today's roughly 50-50 split between the Pacific and the Atlantic to about a 60-40 split between those oceans,", the number of deployed warships in the Pacific will be nearly the same in 2020 because total number of warships are declining. This information means that US power has been declining for the last 23 years and in theory, declining power leads to a power vacuum.

Since the last 23 years, China has been modernizing their navy. The white paper of the Defence of Japan points out that the nominal size of China's announced national defence budget has more than doubled in over the past five years, and has grown approximately 30-fold over the past 24 years. Further, the focus of China's military modernization is Navy and Air Force. As a result, Chinese Navy has been increasing their capability as "Blue Water Navy". In 1990, China possessed 55 surface combatants. 16 of those 55 are "big surface combatants". By 2012, the total number of surface combatants has grown from 55 to 78 and 37 of those 78 are "big surface combatants". Generally, a big ship can operate in a wider area. As a "Blue Water Navy", the capability of Chinese Navy has been improving considerably. China will possess aircraft carrier by 2012. Their submarine forces have modernized and the number of nuclear submarines has increased from 5 to 10.

Figure 1: US needs Japan and India

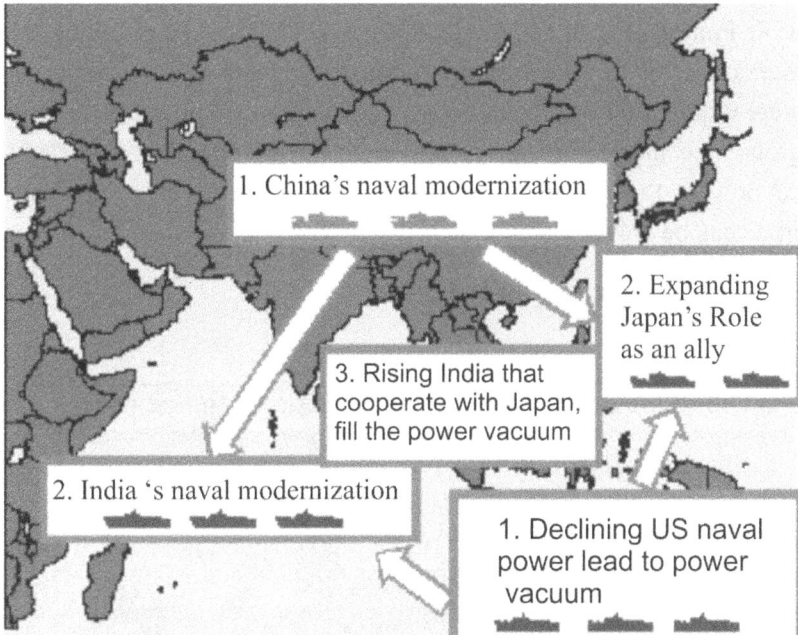

As a result, theoretically it can be said that China's assertiveness in West Pacific and the Indian Ocean reflects power shift in Asia. US needs an ally or a friendly country to fill the power vacuum against China. For example, Mr. Richard L. Armitage, former US deputy secretary of state pointed out that US needs a 'strong Japan' when he published the report "US-Japan Alliance" written by him and Prof. Joseph S. Nye of the Harvard University. As a "Natural Ally "or a "Linchpin", US needs a strong India too. Japan and India are candidates to fill the power vacuum in Asia. Hence, US wants to support the coalition of Japan and India.

ASEAN Needs Japan-India Cooperation

One of the most important questions regarding US-China Power Game is to locate where exactly will "the theatre of the power game" be, in the worst case scenario. To understand this question, we need to know what it takes to qualify as a theatre of a power game. Central Europe included Germany, Poland, Czech Republic, Slovakia, Austria and Hungary etc and was the theatre of the power game in the Cold War. We can image three basic features pertaining to this concept. Firstly, Central Europe is strategically an important place because Europe has been the centre of world politics.

Secondly, Central Europe stood separated as a major military power arena. Thirdly, Central Europe was surrounded by great powers like the erstwhile USSR, France, Britain and United States of America. Thus, taking from this example of Central Europe, it can be concluded that a prominent feature required for an area to become a theatre of the power game is that a group of countries in strategically important places are surrounded by great powers. In the case of Southeast Asia three similarities with Central Europe can be drawn.

Figure 2: Theatre of Power Game

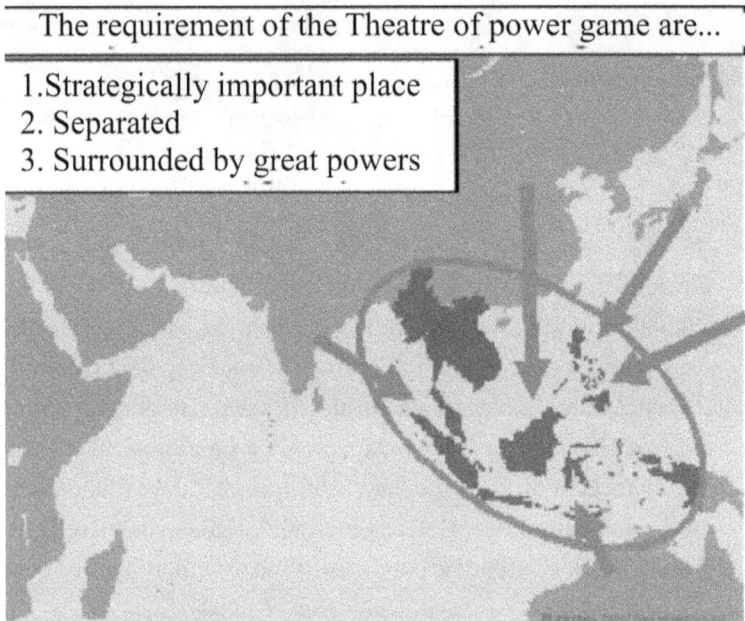

The requirement of the Theatre of power game are...

1. Strategically important place
2. Separated
3. Surrounded by great powers

Strategically Important Place

The region of Southeast Asia is a strategically important area. Southeast Asia is sitting on key Sea Lines of Communication between the Middle East and East Asia. Further, Southeast Asia is a resource rich region. In addition, it provides a good market economically. Thus, Southeast Asia is fulfilling the requirement as a strategically important place.

ASEAN is not an integrated region. Most ASEAN countries have been expanding their navies which imply a certain arms race in the region. Submarines are one symbol of arms race in Asia because submarines cannot carry out military operations other than war. For example, Vietnam ordered 6 new submarines in 2009 first of which they are to receive in late 2012. Malaysia got 2 submarines in 2009. Singapore increased submarines from four to five. Indonesia plans to increase submarines from 2 to 12. Philippine and Thailand's plans to possess submarines, are under consideration.

Figure 3: Arms Race in Southeast Asia

Submarines are one Symbol of arms roce in Asia because submarines Cannot Carry out military operations other than war

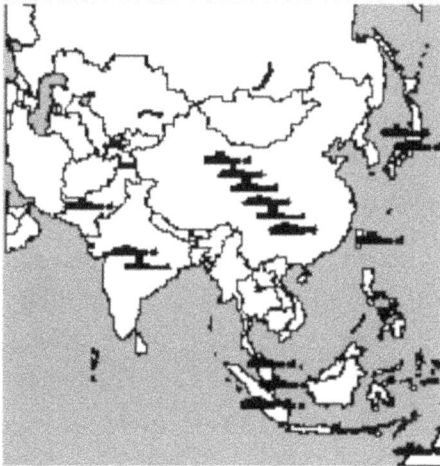

	1990	2010	2020-24
China	94	71	?
Taiwan	4	4	?
Japan	15	18	24
Philippine	0	0	?
Vietnam	0	0	6
Thailand	0	0	?
Malaysia	0	2	?
Singapore	0	5	?
Indonesia	2	2	12
Australia	6	6	12
India	19	15	?
Pakistan	6	5	?

The most important and obvious question that emerges from the above description is why these countries have started modernizing their navy. According to an analysis done in a Jane's Defence Weekly article, these countries want to make sea denial capability to tackle China's naval modernization. Because "sea denial only requires the perception of threat to cause unease in an opponent" and "small numbers of submarines have the potential to deny large areas of sea to an opponent", submarine is the most effective weapon to build sea denial capabilities. If the rationale of submarine modernization is to tackle Chinese naval modernization, it is not a problem because this modernization will symbolize an integrated ASEAN.

However, under an alternative possibility, these countries could need submarines to tackle other fellow ASEAN navies. For example, if Malaysia and Indonesia need submarines to correct military balance with Singapore Navy, this military modernization will lead to a power balancing within ASEAN symbolizing a divided ASEAN. Further, this year, ASEAN cannot conclude Joint Communiqué of the 45th ASEAN Foreign Ministers Meeting because only Hanoi and Manila have proclaimed a strong stance against China's assertiveness.

Surrounded by Great Powers

Southeast Asia is surrounded by great powers like China, Japan, US, Australia and India. Not only China, but other great powers are also modernizing their navies. For example, Japan decided to increase their submarines from 18 to 24 (including 2 for training) in 2010. Australia decided to increase theirs from 6 to 12 despite shortage of crews in 2009. India will increase the number of nuclear submarines from 1 to 4 or 5 in the near future despite decreasing the total number of conventional submarines. And in 2011, US deployed 31 of their 54 nuclear submarines in the Pacific. This US presence is likely to remain unaltered in near future.

Under such situation, ASEAN needs to amalgamate leadership and emerge as one integrated great ASEAN military power. US military power has been playing a role of a stabilizer in Southeast Asia since long. Especially, in the Cold War, US had their base in Thailand and Philippines. Recently, US has again started to show their presence in Southeast Asia. They have concentrated their naval and air power in Guam under Air-Sea battle concept, increased naval exercises, restarted naval assistance to the Philippines, furthered defence relationship with Vietnam, set up new base in Darwin in Australia and will deploy Littoral Combat Ships to Singapore. However, when compared with bases like Subic Bay in Philippines, which was set up by US in the Cold War, new bases located in Darwin and Guam are farther away from China. It appears that China's military modernization has somewhat pushed US military bases further East.

To correct military balance and ensure stability in Southeast Asia, not only US and ASEAN countries, but also allies of the US and other friendly countries including Japan, Australia and India should join together and negotiate with China. Especially, both Japan and India face border issues with China. Hence, Japan-India relations are significantly important in this region.

Japan-India Cooperation

Going by Japan's threat perception, China is the main serious security concern. Ministry of Defence in Japan has specially been concerned about China's military modernization. As per the White Paper *Defence of Japan* "China's response has been criticized as assertive in regards to the issues on conflicting interests with its surrounding countries, including Japan. Thus, there is a concern over its future direction." "Furthermore, China has been expanding and intensifying its activities in its surrounding waters. These moves, together with the lack of transparency in its military affairs and security issues, are a matter of concern for the region and the international community, including Japan, which should require prudent analysis."These strong words in official documents depict the official concern in Japan with respect to China's rising power.

Not only the Ministry of Defence in Japan, but also most Japanese people are concerned about China's rise. The Japan-China joint annual survey conducted by the Genron NPO and the China Daily in 2012, "the ratio of Japanese who had an unfavourable view of China climbed to its highest-ever level of 84.3 per cent"; "The ratio of Chinese who had an unfavourable opinion of Japan slightly improved to 64.5 per cent from 65.9 per cent last year, but it remained above 60 per cent". "When asked about the possibility of a military dispute occurring mainly between Japan and China in the waters of the East China Sea, 50.2 per cent of the Chinese polled, said they foresee such an incident in the near future or in several years. This far surpassed a comparable percentage of 27.2 per cent for the Japanese poles."

Table1: Naval Balance of four countries

	Japan	India	China	US
Aircraft carrier	0	1(+2)	0(+2)	11
(Anti-submarine) helicopter carrier	2(+2)	0	0	0
Destroyer, Frigate, Corvette	46(-2)	46	78	110
Submarine	18	15	71	72
Anti-submarine patrol aircraft	80	9	4	147
Anti-submarine helicopters	88	54	28	255

*Source: International Institute for Strategic Studies Military Balance 2012

Therefore, the argument is to check the military balance in East Asia and the need of the hour is to ponder over its feasibility. In the words of James R Homes, associate professor at the Naval War College "Despite Japan's latter-day image as a military pushover, a naval war would not be a rout for Japan. While the Japanese postwar "peace" constitution forever renounces war as a sovereign right of the nation and the threat or use of force as means of settling international disputes, the Japan Maritime Self-Defence Force (JMSDF) has accumulated several pockets of material excellence, such as under sea warfare, since World War II."

To further elaborate on this point let me substantiate with some examples. Japan possesses two anti-submarine helicopter carriers, 46 anti-submarine destroyers and frigates, 80 P-3C anti-submarine aircraft and 88 anti-submarine helicopters. Compared to India and China, the number of these anti-submarine forces is big. Compared with US Navy, Japan's anti-submarine forces are relatively big despite Japan being significantly smaller than US. The bottom-line of this elaboration was to point out that Japan has worldclass anti-submarine capabilities.

However, there is technical issue involved. To operate these anti-submarine forces except submarines, Japan needs air supremacy too. Japan's 278 fourth generation fighter airplanes will not be enough to tackle China's 522 fourth generation fighters in the near future. Japan cannot increase the number of fighters because the defence budget of Japan has been declining whereas China's defence budget has been increasing considerably.

In addition, the problematic point is that US military budget itself has been declining despite Japan needing additional airpower from the US. Thus, in *The National Military Strategy of United States of America 2011: Redefining America's Military Leadership*, US abandoned "Two major Regional Conflict Strategy" which implied that US should keep the capabilities to defeat enemy when faced with two major regional conflicts occurring nearly simultaneously. Japan is worried about such a scenario when US is faced with a conflict in Southeast Asia or Indian Ocean or Middle East or Africa in addition to providing military support to Japan. To tackle this likelihood, if friendly countries fill the power vacuum as security providers in Southeast Asia and the Indian Ocean, Japan can get full support from US to keep the military balance. Therefore, *National Defence Guideline Program* which decides the direction of Japan's defence policy made in 2010 points out that "Japan will enhance cooperation with India".

India's Importance as a Security Provider

Above all, US, ASEAN and Japan need India as a stabilizing force. There are three potentialities in favour of India becoming a responsible security provider in Asia.

Geographical Potential as a Stabilizer

First potentiality is geographical potential. Historically, three centres of power have dominated the sub-continent, the Mauryan Empire, the Mughal Empire and the British Raj. These three Empires could not project their land power far beyond South Asia because India is surrounded by high mountains. However, as a naval power, the influential area of the Chola Empire could extend to Southeast Asia. The history of Chola Empire has indicated that strategic connection between India and Southeast Asia existed long ago. This means that India has the potential as a security provider in Southeast Asia geographically.

Figure 4: Geographical potentiality of India

The History has Proved that the Location has a Potential as Security Provider in Southeast Asia

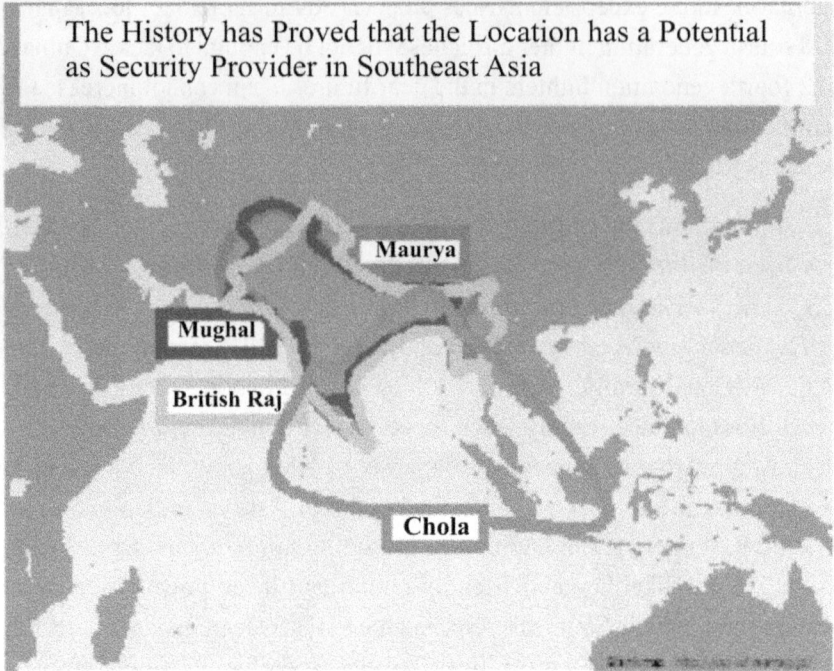

Possessing enough naval power as a security provider

Secondly, India will possess enough naval power to be projected as a strong naval power in the future. For example, the number of "big surface combatants" whose load displacement is more than 3000t has been increasing rapidly in the Indian Navy. Generally, big ship can operate in a wider area than smaller ones. As a "Blue Water Navy", the capability of Indian Navy is improving rapidly.

Figure 5: The number of surface combatants

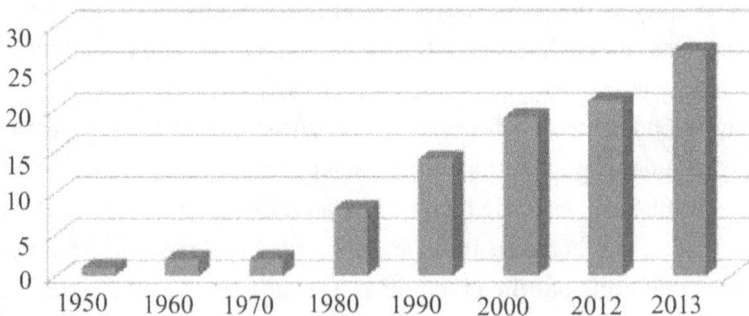

*The load displacement is more than 3000t in the Indian Navy

Trustworthy Partners

There are two reasons as to why India is perceived as a trustworthy partner by most countries except China and Pakistan. When we try to understand military strategy of other countries, we collect information by not only reading official documents but also by exchanging opinions between experts in and out of governments. Freedom of expression in India proves that experts can voice their complaints against government institutions freely. Thus, people can trust these experts in India.

Secondly, because India has exercised restrain to use military power as a strategy in the past, most countries can trust India.Below is given a list of India's military operations. This list proves that most of India's operations are *reactive* and Indian army have not crossed border since 1972 except for peace keeping or peace building operations. India's restraint to use force is a consistent strategy. For most countries, India's perception is that of a trustworthy country.

Table 2: The list of India's Military Operations:

	Active or Reactive	Type of Operation	Area of Operation
Junagadh (1947)	Active	Limited war	Outside
India-Pak (1947-48)	Reactive	Limited war	Outside
Hyderabad (1948)	Active	Limited war	Outside
Northeast (1956-now)	Reactive	Counterinsurgency	Inside
Goa (1961)	Active	Limited war	Outside
India-China (1962)	Reactive	Limited war	Inside
Kutch (1965)	Reactive	Limited war	Inside
India-Pak (1965)	Reactive	Limited war	Outside
Nathu La &Chola (1967)	Reactive	Limited war	Inside
Maoist (1967-now)	Reactive	Counterinsurgency	Inside
India-Pak (1971)	Active	Limited war	Outside
Siachen (1984)	Active	Limited war	Inside
Falcon & Checker-board (1986-87)	Reactive	Coercive diplomacy	Inside
Punjab (1984-92)	Reactive	Counterinsurgency	Inside
Brasstack (1987)	Active	Coercive diplomacy	Inside
Sri Lanka (1987-90)	Active	Peace building	Outside
Maldives (1988)	Reactive	Peace building	Outside
Kashmir (1989-now)	Reactive	Counterinsurgency	Inside
1990Crisis(1990)	Reactive	Coercive diplomacy	Inside
Kargil(1999)	Reactive	Limited war	Inside
Parakram(2001-02)	Reactive	Coercive diplomacy	Inside
UNPKO	Reactive	Peace keeping	Outside

India is an important partner for Japan

Finally, deducing from the arguments presented above, it can be concluded as to why Japan needs India as security provider in the current Asian scenario? Firstly because we need to fill the power vacuum made by declining US power. Secondly Japan and ASEAN *alone* do not have enough power to fill the power vacuum. Thirdly India has potential to become a trustworthy security provider. Thus, to keep the military balance in Asia, India's implementation of a rapid military modernization is hope for Japan. With US, Australia and ASEAN, Japan and India need to cooperate to fill the vacuum to stabilize Asia.

However, there is still one question. Does India have the required will? Japan is waiting for India to show up as a great power in the world.

Session-III

Panel-2

Chairperson

Air Chief Marshal SP Tyagi, PVSM, AVSM, VM (Retd)

First of all on behalf of the panellists , I would like to thank USI for providing us the opportunity. The topic for this session is "Future Security Challenges and Opportunities". You have already heard in the morning session, the views of our distingushed scholars. In this session, we would listen to the opinion of South Korea, Japan, Taiwan and India. As you see we have a very distingushed panel here, and we hope we will be enriched with their thoughts. Without much delay, I would like to request Dr. Daesung Song to present his paper and I request all the panellists to present their views within ten minutes each.

Session-III

Panel-2

First Paper

Dr. Daesung Song

Military Modernization and Its Impact on the Asia-Pacific-Region

Introduction

As McDevitt suggests, there are two forms of military modernization: (1) replacing an old system with a similar new system and (2) adopting entirely new capabilities. In addition there are at least three major operational areas of military modernization: (1) offensive, (2) defensive, and (3) multi-role.

Defensive modernizations are generally stability inducing. Offensive modernizations, on the other hand, can create instability because they are adopted in order to make preparations to attack another country. For example, North Korea's development of a ballistic missile programme is an offensive modernization, which could potentially be used to attack South Korea or neighbouring countries. With multi-role modernizations, which have both offensive and defensive characteristics, it is more difficult to determine the intentions of the nation which has adopted the capability, for example, cyber-warfare capabilities. Thus, military modernization can be defined as an effort made by a nation to update pre-existing military capabilities or to adopt new military capabilities, which may have a defensive, offensive or multi-role orientation.

The Asia-Pacific-Region has many major economic and military powers that both confront one another and cooperate at the same time. The major regional powers maintain mutually cooperative activities while competing with one another in order to secure a dominant position in the region. Solidifying its security ties with major Asia-Pacific alliances

South Korea, Japan, Australia, and the United States have been trying to establish a more effective multilateral security system within the region based on alliances. China and Russia or China and North Korea have been strengthening their strategic partnership. The Shanghai Cooperation Organization (SCO), formed under the leadership of China and Russia. China and Russia agreed to enhance cooperation of their comprehensive strategic partnership during the newly inaugurated Russian President Vladimir Putin's three-day visit to China.

This paper is structured as follows. First, the current military modernization efforts of China, Taiwan, Japan, South Korea, North Korea, and ASEAN (Association of South East Asian Nations) countries, the United States, India and Pakistan will be presented and related to each other. These countries have been selected because they are the major economic, military, and political powers in the region. Emphasis will be placed on the military modernization efforts the strategies and intentions of each country, and the impacts of military modernization on the future security challenges and opportunities in the Asia-Pacific-Region.

Military Modernization Efforts

CHINA

Military Modernization Efforts: Military Expenditure and Capabilities

China has been making a clear effort to modernize its military from as early as the 1990s. This can be seen in the double-digit growth of China's defence spending. China currently ranks second in the world in terms of military expenditure. China's official military budget for 2010 was approximately US$78.6 billion and US$91.5 billion for 2011, indicating a 12.7% increase. SIPRI estimates China's military expenditure to be US$110.1 billion in 2009 and US$114.3 billion in 2010 (using 2009 price levels). In 2009, China's military expenditure is estimated to be 2.2% of GDP. The US Department of Defence estimates China's military expenditure could have been over US$150 billion in 2009 and US$160 billion in 2010. The variation in statistics stems from the lack of transparency in China's expenditure reporting coupled with variations in methods for calculating military expenditure. Nevertheless, China's military expenditure trends do demonstrate that China is making a significant effort to modernize its military.

China's defence spending increases have been put towards modernizing its military in both defensive and offensive areas. First, China is working on the development of ballistic and cruise missiles. It is in the process of testing offensive missiles procured in large part from Russia, and it is working on the development of counter ballistic missile defence systems, and upgrading other missile systems. China's naval capabilities have greatly improved. Significant developments include: a new naval base at Yulin, a new nuclear-powered ballistic missile submarine and expansion of other attack submarines, research and development for an aircraft carrier which could be fully operational by 2015, improved radar systems, domestically produced surface combatants, and the deployment of catamaran hull missile patrol boats. Advancements have also been made in air defence forces which include: newer and more advanced aircraft and placement of combat aircraft within unrefueled range of Taiwan with airfield capacity to expand the number. China has enhanced its ground forces largely in areas of potential conflict with Taiwan including: new battle tanks, amphibious assault vehicles, the first Group Army-level exercise and development of multiple rockets launch systems. China is developing space, counterspace and cyber warfare capabilities. These developments include: a record 15 Space launches in 2010, the development of the Long March V rocket capable of delivering payloads in space, enhancement of space based intelligence and surveillance, and possible development of cyber intrusion and data collection techniques. The US government's computer system among others was intruded in 2010, which seems to have originated in China. Finally, in the area of defence technology acquisition, China is using foreign technology, domestic research and development and illegal intelligence gathering techniques to modernize its military. In sum, the US Department of Defence finds that, "the PLA is on track to achieve its goal of building a modern, regionally focused military by 2020." While the growth of China's military spending is alarming, particularly among its regional neighbours, China's military expenditure is quite small in comparison to the military expenditure of the United States at present. China's extensive military modernization effort is in part a corollary of rapid economic growth. Thus, one must be cautious when examining the extent of and intentions of

China's military modernization.

Strategies and Intensions

Finkelstein notes that there are 3 pillars of PLA reforms: (1) the development of new military capabilities, (2) institutional and systematic changes which include improved professionalism and other changes to corporate culture and (3) the development of new war fighting doctrines. As Finkelstein analysis suggests, China's military modernization goes beyond simply developing new capabilities. It encompasses institutional reforms and the development of new military strategies. Furthermore, the thrust for modernization of the PLA can be discerned from China's "Military Strategic Guidelines for the New Period". China's overall military strategy is defensive where China will only attack after being attacked. At the same time, China considers its operations as offensive. Finkelstein speculates that the main direction of China's military strategy is centred upon preventing threat of Taiwanese independence.

Despite China's increasing military expenditure, military modernization efforts, and security guidelines, which indicate an offensive military orientation, China states in its White Paper that it will continue "on the path of peaceful development"? The paper goes on to indicate that China pursues a policy, which is "defensive in nature" and "China will never seek hegemony, nor will it adopt the approach of military expansion". However, China's stance towards Taiwan and also Tibet and East Turkistan seem to contradict these principles. The White Paper goes on to state that one of China's major goals and tasks is to "oppose and contain the separatist forces of 'Taiwan independence,' crack down on separatist forces for 'East Turkistan independence' and 'Tibet independence,' and defend national sovereignty and territorial integrity."

The strategies and intensions of China's military modernization efforts put forth in China's public official statements are riddled with contradictions and fail to make the modern development of China's military a transparent process. Thus, even though China has attempted to emphasize its peaceful intentions, other nations in the Asia-Pacific-Region have increased their own military expenditures and their modernization effort in response to China's growing military power.

TAIWAN

Military Modernization Efforts: Military Expenditure and Capabilities

In early 2011, Taiwan's Ministry of National Defence stated that it would not engage in an arms race with China despite China's double-digit increase in military spending. Instead the ministry suggested that it would place emphasis on making optimal use of its own defence budget. From 2006 to 2009 Taiwan's military expenditure grew from US$7.419 billion to US$9.008 billion then fell to US$8.535 billion in 2010. Taiwan's military expenditure as a percentage of GDP increased from 1.9% in 2006 to 2.4 % in 2009 but fell in 2010.

Taiwan's defence budget from 2002 to 2011 was between NT $250 billion and NT $330 billion, which was between 15.52% and 19.51% of the central government's total budget. This demonstrates that despite economic downturn due to economic crisis, the defence budget represents a fairly significant portion of total government spending. In 2011 Taiwan's defence budget was NT$294.58 billion. Furthermore, Taiwan aims to keep its military spending at or above 3% of GDP in order to reach its military modernization goals.

Taiwan's military modernization efforts are centred upon: establishing defence capabilities, promoting an all-volunteer force, strengthening non-combat capabilities such as consolidating national identity, procurement of necessary weapons (including those bought from the US), enhancing cooperation with allies, and improving benefits for military personnel. Taiwan's effort to modernize its military has been fraught with financial difficulty. The global financial crisis, foreign arms procurement and the financial demands of transition to an all-volunteer force have put significant strain on Taiwan's modernization plans.

Strategy and Intentions

Taiwan summarizes that the purpose of its military strategy is to, "defend national security, prepare for but not seek war; absolutely not provoke or launch attacks; and abide by international norms against developing nuclear weapons or other weapons of mass destruction."

The Ma Ying-Jeou administration has emphasized Taiwan's intentions to maintain peace and stability while also acknowledging clear security threats from China. These threats remain an important factor in Taiwan's strengthening impetus for military modernization. Taiwan's National Defence Report 2011 notes that since 2003 the PLA has been using a non-military "three warfare's" strategy where public opinion, psychological and legal methods are being used to thwart Taiwan. China also has not renounced its will to attack Taiwan with force if Taiwan declares independence. In addition, China's military modernization efforts have been made with a focus on possible conflicts with Taiwan. Finally, Taiwan's Quadrennial Defence Review notes that China's military growth lacks transparency leading to security uncertainties.

JAPAN

Military Modernization Efforts: Military Expenditure Capabilities

Japan's military expenditure as a percentage of GDP has remained at approximately 1% for decades now. This reflects the legacy of the post-WWII order and strong anti-military sentiment domestically.

First, Japan is modernizing its military capabilities enhancing the mobility of its Ground Self-Defence Force (GSDF), Maritime Self Defence Force (MSDF) and Air-Self Defence Force (ASDF) to more quickly reach offshore islands and other distant areas. Japan is working to develop MSDF amphibious and carrier technologies, and new fighter aircraft units. It will maintain augmented submarine units, fixed-wing patrol aircraft, minesweeper units and air-warning control units, and surface to air-guided missile units. It is also enhancing joint operations, improving intelligence-gathering capabilities, improving the efficiency of equipment procurement, and promoting research and development especially in aerospace and cyber defence areas. Some scholars suggest that Japan may be engaging in a "quiet arms race" with China. Hughes suggests, "Japan is in many cases engaged in something of a quiet arms race with China: matching Chinese growing air power with its own enhanced air defensive power; countering Chinese growing blue-water naval ambitions with its own more capable anti-submarine and carrier assets; and attempting to nullify Chinese ballistic and cruise missiles."

Strategy and Intensions

Japan continues to emphasize that it will only maintain a defence-oriented military and will not attempt to become a threatening military power to other countries, as mentioned in Article 9 of Japan's Constitution. At the same time, Japan has perceived heightened security threats from both China's rapid military modernization and North Korea's continual brinkmanship strategy. Japan's National Defence Program Guidelines state, "the global shift in the balance of power is apparent in the Asia-Pacific-Region," citing the North Korea's nuclear weapons programme and the military modernization efforts of neighbouring countries, particularly China. Thus, Japan has responded by increasingly pursuing efforts for the long-term modernization of its military forces. Japan will also no longer use its traditional concept of defence, "Basic Defence Force Concept," which implies deterrence through defence forces. Rather, it will use the concept of, "Dynamic Defence Force," implying that Japan's defence forces will be more versatile, mobile, ready, sustainable and flexible.

SOUTH KOREA

Military Modernization Efforts: Military Expenditure and Capabilities

South Korea's military expenditure remains high but relatively constant due to the continued tensions on the Korean peninsula. South Korea's military expenditure has risen from US$24.182 billion in 2008 to US$ 25.069 billion in 2010. As a percentage of GDP South Korea's military expenditure fell from a high of 4.5% in 1998 to a low of 2.5% in 2002, then began to gradually rise again to 2.9% by the end of 2009. This increase reflects South Korea's willingness to have a more self-reliant military.

Since the Roh Mu Hyun administration (2003-2008), South Korea has sought to rely less on US military presence and focus more on developing its own capabilities. South Korea's Defence Reform 2020 highlighted South Korea's intended areas of military modernization.South Korea plans for advanced weapons procurement and the upgrading over the next 5 years or so. However; considering budget constraints these ambitious plans are unlikely to be realized without proper prioritization. The 2020 reform plans have since been revised by the Lee Myung-Bak administration. South Korea plans continue to build up its reserve forces despite its declining birth-rate. The country also plans to improve military mobilization by restructuring its reserve forces. South Korea has developed modern aircraft and surface-to-air missiles. South Korea also has plans for a "blue water" navy to protect its maritime interests. In addition, it has a strong aero-space and shipbuilding industry with rigorous research and development programmes. South Korea plans to modernize its military in preparation for network-centric warfare. While Korea plans to become self-reliant force in the future, at present it relies on US presence in the region. In the case of war the US has committed to provide 690,000 troops and 2,000 warplanes.

Strategy and Intensions

Korea's national security objectives are to ensure security and to maintain peace and stability on the Korean Peninsula. Korea's national security strategy has three tenets: "creating a new peace structure," "carrying out pragmatic diplomacy and openness," and "seeking advanced security that reaches out to the world." South Korea's impetus for military reforms continues to derive primarily from the threat of North Korea. However, growing attention is being paid to China's rapid military modernization and its contention with Taiwan.

NORTH KOREA

Military Modernization Efforts: Military Expenditure and Capabilities

Military expenditure data regarding North Korea is only available in rough estimation due to the country's taciturn political stance. North Korea has reported its military spending to be approximately US$570 million in 2009. However, the Korea Institute for Defence Analysis (KIDA) estimates that it was roughly US$8.77 billion in 2009. North Korea has released that its military spending rose from US$510 million in 2007 to US$540 million in 2008 and then to US$570 million in 2009. Also in 2009, KIDA estimated that North Korea's GNI was around 28.6 trillion Korean Won or approximately (US$25 billion). The US Department of State, in 2009, found that out of a GDP of US$40 billion, 22% was spent on defence unlike the 15.8% reported by North Korea. These figures suggest that North Korea's military expenditure is significantly disproportionate to its social welfare expenditure, while its total pool of funds remains stifled by its flailing economy.

North Korea maintains the world's fourth-largest standing armed forces. It has an active duty military force of 1.19 million. In terms of man power the North Korea's military surpasses the South with about 655,000 active duty members. However, North Korea significantly falls behind South Korea in terms of military technological capability. North Korea's military modernization has emphasized the expansion of its forces rather than on modernization of its military equipment. Resources have been poured into development of long-range missiles and biological, chemical and nuclear weapons. North Korea's long-range missiles include: Nodong (1,300km range), Taepodong-1 (1,500km range) and Taepodong-2 (6,000km range). North Korea has conducted two nuclear tests one on 09 October 2006 and second on 25 May 2009. Some estimate that North Korea may have obtained enough plutonium to hold 4 to13 nuclear weapons. North Korea's most recent provocative acts include second nuclear test, the testing of Taepodong-2 missile in April 2009 and launching a long-range rocket (the Kwang-myongsung-3) on 13 April 2012, its sinking of the South Korean ship the Cheonan in March 2010 and the bombing of Yeonpyeong Island in November 2010. Thus, North Korea remains a formidable threat, which could quickly and unexpectedly destabilize the region.

Strategy and Intensions

North Korea's military strategy is a carefully calculated brinkmanship policy to maximize its bargaining power in negotiations with international powers while minimizing threats to regime collapse by emphasizing the continued development of its military power. North Korea's military first policy characterizes all facets of North Korean society, economy, and politics. This policy is to accomplish its foremost political goals of regime survival and the reunification of the Korean peninsula. North Korea's military first policy has been the most valuable political philosophy for the former-leader Kim Jong-il and the current leader Kim Jong-un. The key contentions of the policy are: (1) North Korean military power is the fundamental power to communize the entire Korean peninsula-unification under North Korean communist control; (2) its military power is the security power to protect the North Korean regime; (3) its power is the biggest bargaining power for

North Korean national interests.

North Korea maintains that the Korean peninsula is still in a state of war and accordingly keeps its military in a perpetual state of full mobilization. Therefore, North Korea puts the majority of its efforts and scarce resources into the development of its military strength. In particular, North Korea's development of weapons of mass destruction remains a critical source of North Korea's bargaining power in international negotiations.

North Korea's military strategy goes hand in hand with its guiding ideological principle of Juche, which is often translated in English to mean self-reliance. Juche serves as the theoretical underpinning of North Korea's military strategy. In Kim IL Sung's work, "On the Juche Idea", Kim states that (1) independence in politics, (2) self-sufficiency in the economy, and (3) self-reliance in defence are the fundamental principles for upholding North Korea's Juche ideology. Self- reliance in defence entails: a defence system incorporating all people of the country, the modernization of the army, and the cultivation of revolutionary devotion of the army, a self-reliant national defence industry, arming all the people and fortifying the country. Each of these elements is seen as essential to maintaining an independent sovereign state. Thus it is this strategy of self-reliant defence that North Korean regime sees as imperative for self-maintenance.

An important area of concern remains the shift of power from Kim Jong-Il to his son Kim Jong-Un, which makes North Korea's future strategies and intensions more uncertain. Also, to ensure the stability of the regime during the transition of power, some scholars have insisted that North Korea is attempting to unify domestic sentiments by creating a commonly perceived external threat to North Korea. These tactics legitimize North Korea's military first policy as well as the regimes power. This can be seen in the two most recent incidents involving South Korea: the torpedoing of the South Korean ship the Cheonan and the Yeonpyeong Island attack.

ASEAN MEMBER COUNTRIES

Military Modernization Efforts: Military Expenditure and Capabilities

In aggregate terms, by 2011, ASEAN military expenditure had reached approximately US$25 billion per year. ASEAN countries' military expenditure as percentage of GDP has remained relatively stable and even declined since 2003 with the exception of Thailand and Singapore.

Despite the setbacks of the 1997 Asian Financial Crisis, ASEAN countries have been making an increasingly concerted effort to modernize their military capabilities. As Bitzinger suggests, Southeast Asia is rearming in response to China's rising military power and also in response to other international and domestic security concerns. Many countries have taken modernization efforts beyond simply replacing old equipment to acquiring new advanced capabilities. Particularly countries with established defence industries including Indonesia, Malaysia, Singapore and Thailand have made efforts to modernize their militaries. They have developed new capabilities including: command and control, force projection, precision strike and surveillance that they did not posses few years ago.

Both Malaysia and Indonesia have expressed interest in promotion of ASEAN Defence Industry Collaboration (ADIC). This would involve production and procurement of weapons within ASEAN nations rather than importing weapon systems from outside of the Association. The goal is to reduce defence imports to US $12.5 billion by 2030. Indonesia's plan is to be self-sufficient by 2030. This effort indicates a greater willingness to collaborate in defence areas. However, the ADIC remains in initial stage and as such has minimal impact on the military modernization efforts of individual ASEAN members.

Strategy and Intensions

ASEAN nations collectively are devoted to the maintenance of peaceful development in the South East Asian region. ASEAN countries have strong geo-political significance in the region and are highly endowed with natural resource. Hence the region remains an area of strategic interest. At the same time, ASEAN countries have been enhancing economic relations with other nations in the region particularly via export of raw materials to China. Since the launch of FTA with China in 2003, ASEAN trade with China has increased annually on an average of 26%. As of 2009, ASEAN was China's 4th largest trading partner. There remain a number of border disputes with countries neighbouring China including the Spratly and Parcel Islands. ASEAN countries are currently in the process of weighing the costs and benefits of cooperation with China. They remain skeptical of China's military modernization intentions and in response have hastened their military modernization efforts while appeasing China in other areas to maintain economic relations.

UNITED STATES

Military Modernization Efforts: Military Expenditure and Capabilities

Since11 September 2001 terrorist attacks and subsequent wars in Afghanistan and Iraq the United States military expenditure has almost doubled from US$378.925 billion in 2001 to US$693.600 billion in 2010. Military expenditure as a percentage of GDP has risen from 3 per cent in 1999 to 4.7 per cent in 2010. Furthermore, the United States military expenditure is greater than the combined expenditure of the next 17 highest ranked countries in terms of military expenditure.

The US military remains the most powerful military in the world. The US finds that it must improve its capabilities in six areas. These are defence of the US and civil authorities, counterinsurgency, stability, and counterterrorism operations, building the security capacity of partner states, deterring aggression in anti-access environment, preventing proliferation of weapons of mass destruction and improving cyberspace capabilities. Key capabilities that the US would like to acquire include: rotary-wing aircraft, unmanned aircraft systems, intelligence analysis and foreign language expertise, and tactical communication networks, more effective space-based assets and electronic attack systems, and better infrastructure. The flexibility and adaptability of forces is a key area to reform. One of the major factors justifying modernization is to ensure that the US maintains its competitiveness in light of China's developing capabilities in the areas of modern navel and aerospace technologies, which are likely to be significant areas of future conflict.

However, economic recession in the US as well as the United State's exorbitant government debt are likely to take a toll on the United States military expenditure and military modernization efforts. In terms of East Asian regional security, it will be critical for the United States to prioritize its defence budget and allocate sufficient funds to ensure the strength of its military in the East Asian region, to counter - balance the rise of China.

Strategy and Intensions

The US finds that, "America's interests and role in the world require Armed Forces with unmatched capabilities and a willingness on the part of the nation to employ them in defence of national interests and the common good." This seemingly implies the US seeks to keep its capabilities apace with other nations in order to achieve its national interests and security. Thus, the US seeks to continue developing its military capabilities in order to maintain its military power position.

Under the Barack Obama administration, a renewed emphasis has been placed on US foreign policy in East Asia. To begin with, US Secretary of State, Hillary Clinton's inaugural visit abroad in 2009 was made to East Asia rather than the Middle East, symbolically indicating the United States renewed interests in East Asia in the 21st century. The US does find China's opaque military development troubling and seeks to enhance military-to-military coordination with China. Thus, the US has worked to strengthen its "bed-rock" alliances in East Asia with most notably, Japan, South Korea, Australia, the Philippines, and Thailand. At the same time, the US remains pre-occupied with its wars in Afghanistan and Iraq and with the economic recession, somewhat deriding its efforts in East Asia.

INDIA

Military Modernization Efforts: Military Expenditure and Capabilities

India's military expenditure has increased from US$22.557 billion in 2001 to US$34.816 billion in 2010. India's military expenditure as percentage of GDP decreased from 3.1% in 1999 to 2.3% in 2007, which is partially a reflection of India's economic growth. However, it has since increased to 2.8% in 2009.

Between 2006 and 2010, India exceeded China as the world's largest importer of arms. India plans to spend an estimated US$80 billion on military modernization by 2015. India's modernization plans have highlighted the necessity of developing weapons manufacturing capabilities domestically. India is currently developing a nuclear submarine and attempting to procure two additional aircraft carriers. India also launched its first unmanned moon mission in October 2008 suggesting a space race with China and other countries. Some, however; criticize that India is "arming without aiming" which implies that India has failed to properly prioritize its military modernization needs. If this is the case it could have serious implications for the military balance of power in the region.

Strategy and Intensions

India is making efforts to modernize its military as a result of rapid economic growth and also due to continued security threats from Pakistan involving disputed region of Jammu and Kashmir. India has traditional border disputes with China. China continues to maintain close diplomatic relations with Pakistan and even supplies arms to Pakistan causing concern for India. Some speculate that China has even given nuclear technology to Pakistan. In response, India has also been working to enhance cooperation with the United States. US President Barack Obama visited India in 2010 in order to enhance bilateral ties between the two nations.

PAKISTAN

Military Modernization Efforts: Military Expenditure and Capabilities

Pakistan's military expenditure as a percentage of GDP has gradually declined from 6.1% in 1992 to 2.8% in 2009. Pakistan's military expenditure has gradually risen from US$3.798 billion in 1997 to US$5.160 billion in 2010. These trends illustrate Pakistan's military budgetary challenges.

Pakistan has the world's eighth largest military. However, at the same time Pakistan has been faced with budget setbacks as well as sanctions, which could threaten to diminish Pakistan's military power and modernization efforts. Therefore, in terms of economics, population, equipment, and manpower size, Pakistan lags behind India.

The US was providing Pakistan aid to modernize its military. However, after 1990 with the discovery of Pakistan's nuclear weapons programme sanctions were implemented. In 2001, the US agreed to resume aid to Pakistan in exchange for its intelligence and military operations in the war in Afghanistan. Beginning in 2005, the US gave Pakistan economic and military aid worth US$3 billion for five years. In 2010, another US$2 billion dollar package was pledged, though the US has threatened to revoke this aid package in 2011 due to provocative developments of nuclear weapons. Despite Pakistan's budgetary setbacks it has continued to develop nuclear arsenal. Pakistan is in the process of building a fourth nuclear reactor. US intelligence experts suggest that Pakistan has 95 to 110 deployed nuclear weapons. Pakistan could soon have the 5th largest nuclear arsenal in the world, putting it ahead of both Britain and India.

Strategy and Intensions

Pakistan has felt pressure from India's rapid military modernization efforts. It has continued to align itself with China and seeks to deter pressure from India over Jammu and Kashmir. Pakistan and the US have collaborated when convenient for both parties. However, Pakistan has been adopting a double face in its dealing, causing the US to periodically stop aid programme to Pakistan.

Impact of Military Modernization on the Future Security Challenges and Opportunities in the Asia Pacific Region

CHINA

The increase in China's economic strength and cooperation, in the Asia-Pacific-Region, with its neighbouring countries is the factor that sustains peace and stability and prevents the security tension issue from escalating to a serious stage.

China's "Military Modernization", and economic growth, is increasing instability and tension in the Asia-Pacific-Region. In reality it is a competition between China and the US for hegemony in the Asia-Pacific-Region.

The neighbouring countries perceive China's military modernization as increase in China's offensive capabilities. So the neighbouring countries are trying to increase their own military capacity. Therefore, China's military modernization is a factor that increases its neighbour's military capacity and heightens instability and tension in the Asia-Pacific-Region.

China's major goal is, "oppose and contain the separatist forces of 'Taiwan independence', crack down on separatist forces for 'East Turkistan independence' and 'Tibet independence' (Strong Military Intervention) is internationally being linked to "human rights issues". This kind of linkage is creating tension against the Western World, including the US. As a result; it is becoming a factor that also creates tension in the Asia-Pacific-Region.

China's military growth and its collisions with other countries in the South-China Sea is increasing insecurity among China and other Southeast Asian countries. And this is giving US an opportunity to actively intervene in Asia. This is a major factor for creating tension in the Asia-Pacific-Region.

China's unreasonable support and protection of North Korea is not only hindering the opportunity to create a change in the North Korean regime significantly but also contributing to North Korea's efforts to develop WMDs. Additionally, China's support is increasing the tension between North and South Korea. Finally, China's unreasonable protection of North Korea is also creating huge tension in Northeast Asia, especially when it comes to the US support for its ally, South Korea.

TAIWAN

Despite increase in China's military capacity, Taiwan has declared that it would not engage in an arms race with China. Taiwan's policy regarding China is reducing the Taiwan-China tension and increasing peace prospects between the two nations. However, if China aggressively pursues unification with Taiwan or Taiwan declares independence, the tension has a high possibility of surfacing.

JAPAN

Japan's "change in its own defence force concept" (from "Basic" defence force concept to "Dynamic" defence force concept) and "quiet arms race with China" are the main factors that have facilitated Northeast Asia's arms race. It can be said that the motive of Japan's increased military capacity is a reaction to China's increased military capacity. Japan's increased military capacity is creating tension and collision between the two countries as is evident due to eruption of disputes with China regarding Senkaku Island and against Korea regarding Dokdo Island. This "tension escalation" between Japan and China, could get the US involved in the Asia-Pacific-Region, because of the alliance between the US and Japan.

SOUTH KOREA

The continued tension on the Korean Peninsula and the provocations by North Korea are becoming a major factor that escalates the Korean Peninsula's tensions and increases the arms race in the Northeast Asia Region. It is also creating tension and conflict between South and North Korea, between South Korea and China, between North Korea and the US and finally between the US and China.

South Korea feels a serious threat from China's rapid increase in its military capacity because China is unreasonably supporting North Korea. This kind of serious security threat the South Koreans are facing is strengthening the South Korea's resolve to secure its military capacity. And the result is a military build-up in both South and North Korea. China's unreasonable support towards North Korea is a factor of Asia-Pacific-Region's conflict and tense situation.

The military capacity of South Korea and the US forces in South Korea is mainly designed for South Korea's national defence. However; after 2010, in other words since North Korea's unilateral attack on South Korean Navy corvette "Cheonan" and Yeonpyeong Island, the public is criticizing the South Korean military's weakness in deterrence capability. The retaliation capability has gained strength domestically. As a result, through the modification: "Military Reformation 2020", President Lee Myung-bak is conducting a reformation of its military capacity by strengthening deterrence and its retaliation capacity. South Korea's enhanced capacity regarding military deterrence and retaliation will contribute to reducing North Korea's armed provocations. But there is a possibility that this can be a factor that increases Northeast Asia's military build-up.

South Korea needs to continue the "ROK-US Combined Defence System", which provides extended deterrence of the US military, due to South Korea'sWMDs inadequacies. The necessity of ROK-US Combined Defence System is strengthening the US Armed Forces in South Korea. Thus ROK-US Alliance is making the struggle for leadership, between the US and China, in the Asia-Pacific-Region more severe. The most significant contributors, when it comes to the U.S involvement in the Asia-Pacific-Region, are North Korea and China.

NORTH KOREA

The fact that North Korea exists on the Korean Peninsula means that there is an "explosive house" in Northeast Asia Region. North Korea has been the source of tensions and conflicts in Northeast Asia and the Asia-Pacific-Region and unless the fundamentals of the North Korean Regime change, this will continue.

North Korea's military first policy has been considered as "the magic mallet of goblin" to solve every difficult issue for North Korea. It is unlikely that North Korea will decrease its military power, nor give up its WMD development programme, and will be the explosive house in Northeast Asia.

North Korea will never give up its WMD development programme under the military first policy. This means that North Korea will become the key factor for conflicts in the Asia-Pacific-Region.

North Korea has continued its unification policy whose goal is to unify the entire Korean Peninsula under communism with military power. This has caused distrust between both Koreas. This North Korean unification policy has become the main source to create conflicts on the Korean Peninsula and in the Asia-Pacific-Region.

ASEAN MEMBER COUNTRIES

The increase in exchange and cooperation among ASEAN countries in the Southeast Asian region can be a factor that increases peace and stability in this area. It also can function as a factor that decreases the tension between them and China.

China's rapid increase in its military capacity is becoming a factor that elevates the insecurity of ASEAN countries. Especially, the military collision between China and ASEAN countries in the South-China Sea is causing military build-up in ASEAN countries. This is becoming a conflict factor in the Southeast Asian region, which has been a relatively stable and quiet region.

UNITED STATES

The US Foreign Policy evaluates Asia and lays stress on East Asia; it will function in two ways. 1) If the US enters into a competition against China, to get hegemony in the Asia-Pacific-Region, it will function as a negative factor towards peace and stability in this area. 2) If the US and China cooperate and build a constructive relationship; it will contribute as a positive factor towards peace and stability in this area. However, these two major powers are intertwined in a complex web of both security and economic agreements, which also serve as a stabilizing force. Mutual interests for peace and stability remain strong.

The US maintains its competiveness in light of China's developing capabilities in the areas of modern naval and aerospace technology. Those are likely to be significant areas of future conflict. If China's naval power was to challenge US naval power in the region, the US would respond by modernizing its own naval fleet in addition to increasing US Naval presence in the Pacific. As Evans argues, "any serious long-term challenge by Beijing to the East Asian maritime status quo would be met by expanded US naval modernization and trigger an arms race." Especially, the competitiveness in the area of naval power between the US and China would be a serious factor for conflict in the Asia-Pacific-Region.

The US effort of strengthening its "bed-rock" alliances in East Asia with most notably, Japan, South Korea, Australia, the Philippines, and Thailand will have the following meaning:-

(a) If China tries to become a reasonable country and put its effort to settle peace and stability in the Asia-Pacific-Region, the US effort of strengthening its alliance in this area will diminish.

(b) If China acts unreasonably or in an opposite way and does not put its true effort to settle peace and stability in the Asia-Pacific-Region (e.g., unreasonably supporting rogue states while trying to get the hegemony in this region), the US alliance with Asian countries in this region is going to be more solid and the competition between the US and China, to gain hegemony in this area is going to become more competitive. As a result, the Asia-Pacific-Region will become a mudslinging battlefield for hegemony or a troubled area.

The US World Strategy (which clearly states, "America's interests and role in the world require Armed Forces with unmatched capabilities and a willingness on the part of the nation to employ them in defence of our national interests and the common good") has greatly contributed for securing stability and peace in the Asia-Pacific-Region. A good example is the US Armed Forces in Korea. For the past 60 years, North Korea, which invaded South Korea and caused the Korean War in 1950, never gave up its goal to unify the Korean Peninsula through its military force. At this moment, North Korea still has the will and capacity to achieve that goal. The reason why North Korea is withholding from using its military force is because the US Armed Forces are stationed in South Korea. Even if China and North Korea perceive the US Armed Forces in South Korea as a factor that creates tension, people who respect the true value of liberal democracy regard them as "Peacekeeping Forces".

INDIA

India's advancement in the high-tech weapon producing industry and entrance into the "star wars" has substantially contributed to her potential as a major power inclusive of military might. India's role to facilitate peace and stability, in the Asia-Pacific-Region will become very important. India has become the world's largest arms importing country. This is due to India's own national defence effort to modernize its military against China and Pakistan. However, this is a factor that promotes the arms build-up in the Asia-Pacific-Region.

The friction between India and Pakistan, including dispute over Jammu and Kashmir could spill over into the region. If China tries to support Pakistan one-sidedly, it is very likely that India will form a strong network with the U.S and have confrontation with them.

PAKISTAN

The fact that there is tension between India and Pakistan, and the fact that the US and China are separately supporting each side and creating a firm network, are factors that can spread the existing tension between India and Pakistan across the whole Asia-Pacific-Region. The current struggle between the US and China to acquire India's friendship can be repeated with Pakistan. And this kind of phenomenon can function as a factor that increases either peace or tension in the Asia-Pacific-Region.

Pakistan and India's competition to develop nuclear weapons is a serious factor that can destroy peace and stability in the Asia-Pacific-Region, along with North Korea's continuous pursuit of nuclear development programmes. This factor has to be controlled under NPT's regulations so that it will not actually destroy peace in the Asia-Pacific-Region. Especially, Pakistan's continuous pursuit of its nuclear development programme and the fact that she already has 95–110 nuclear weapons, can destroy peace in the Asia-Pacific-Region.

SUMMARY AND CONCLUSION

Strengthen Mutual Interests

In order to ensure the stability of the Asia-Pacific-Region, nations must work to strengthen interests in areas outside the security realm. Particularly, strengthened economic ties could lead to strengthened mutual interests. For instance, stronger efforts to establish regional trade agreements and forums such as ASEAN+6 and ASEAN+3 will be important. There is currently no formal regional economic cooperation institution in North East Asia. An institution of this nature could strengthen mutual interests for a stable security environment in the region while at the same time contributes to greater economic stability. However, a critical obstacle to this remains the lack of a unified need for supranational political cooperation in the manner that exists for example in the European Union.

Strengthen Multilateral Security Arrangements and Security Dialogues

At present, a significant regional security forum in the Asia-Pacific-Region is absent. The ASEAN Regional Forum (ARF) stands as the most comprehensive effort to engage all regional players in security dialogue. While, the forum currently remains largely impotent, the strengthening of the forum could serve as a significant multilateral mechanism for regional security.

In addition to formal bilateral and multilateral forums amongst government leaders, East Asian think tanks and both governmental and non governmental organizations, which engage civil society in the security cooperation dialogue, are important.

Open and Transparent Military Modernization

Perhaps the most important factor to ensure stability in the Asia-Pacific-Region will be the increased openness and transparency of nation's military modernization programmes and intensions. One obvious way to improve transparency would be to make more information regarding nation's specific intentions and military development programmes available to the public. While some information is sensitive in nature, enhanced transparency could attenuate neighbouring countries concerns about China's high military expenditure and modernization.

There should be transparency in data collection and publication, and prevent asymmetrical information problems which could lead to grave miscalculations in nation's security policies. If China's efforts are indeed benign then more effective communication of its military capabilities and intensions should be a feasible imperative in the near term. In addition, another way to increase transparency will be to improve military to military dialogues. These dialogues are particularly important between the US and China. These have been hampered recently perhaps due to US continued arms sales to Taiwan.

Increase Complex Inter-dependence Relations

One unique feature of 21st century international politics is 'complex inter-dependence relations'. Every country in the Asia-Pacific-Region has been keeping complex inter-dependence relations. This means that while country A and country B may have conflicts in security issue but they accommodate eachother in say economic cooperation and so on. For example, Korea and Taiwan have accommodated China to some extent. Ross finds that South Korea has accommodated the rise of China by resisting post-Cold War defence cooperation with the United States. However, China and South Korea have been having very strong economic relations, as well as good relations in tourism sector. Taiwan's accommodation of China can be seen as its increasing acceptance of the "one-China principle" or the acknowledgement of Chinese sovereignty over Taiwan. These phenomena seem to suggest that these states may be increasingly finding alignment with

China in some areas beneficial to their security.

Try to Unify the Korean Peninsula

The divided Korean peninsula and the distrust between them have been important factors for unrest in Northeast Asia. The distrust between the two Koreas has created conflicts. Peacekeeping on the Korean Peninsula may be achieved by confidence building measures taken by both the Koreas. Peacekeeping on the Korean peninsula for long, may unite both the Koreas. The unification of the Korean peninsula means: (1) Stability in the Northeast Asian region; (2) Getting rid of confrontational structure between South Korea and the US and North Korea and China; (3)The relations between the unified Korea and China will become interdependent.

Respect 'World Opinion'

A more deliberate dialogue concerning deep-seated historical and territorial disputes between nations in the Asia-Pacific-Region is necessary. For example, Korea-Japan relations remain stifled due to issues surrounding Japan's colonization of Korea in the 20th century. Korean and Japanese textbooks represent historical events in a different light creating a point of contention between the two countries. There is territorial dispute ranging from naming of Korea and Japan's shared sea as the East Sea or Sea of Japan, to disputed claim of the Dokdo Islands. A continued dialogue regarding these issues could serve to resolve obstacles and pave the way for further cooperation.

Keep Strategic Dialogues between the US and China

One of the special features of the security environment in Northeast Asia is that the United States and China are members of G2 and have been cooperating sometimes, but have also been causing complications. The cooperation between the G2 has brought a peaceful security environment and conflicts between them has made the security environment unstable. The countries in Northeast Asia have been heavily influenced by the relationship of these two G2 countries.

In order to have peace and security in the Asia-Pacific-Region we need to have strategic dialogue between US and China. Both countries should try to transform conflicting issues through reconcilliation. "China and the

US should cooperate more closely to defuse international crises and ensure friction does not overwhelm shared interests."

Bibliography

1. "Annual Report to Congress: Military and Security Developments Involving the People's Republic of China 2011" US Department of Defence, 2011.

2. Bitzinger, Richard A. "The China Syndrome: Chinese Military Modernization and the Rearming of Southeast Asia." Singapore: *S. Rajaratnam School of International Studies.* May 2, 2007.

3. "China's National Defence 2010." *Chinese Government's Official Web Portal gov.cn.*March2011.http://english.gov.cn/official/2011-3/31/content_1835499.htm.

4. Cohen, Stephen P. and Sunil Dasgupta. *Arming Without Aiming: India's Military Modernization.* Brookings Institution Press, 2010.

5. Cordesman, Anthony H. "The Korean Military Balance: Comparative Korean Forces and the Forces of Key Neighbouring States," *CSIS.* February 14, 2011.

6. "Defending the Nation's Sovereignty Expanding Roles in Wider Horizons: Defence White Paper 2011." *Ministry of Defence Brunei Darussalam.* 2011.

7. Evans, Michael. "Power and Paradox: Asian Geopolitics and Sino-American Relations in the 21st Century." *Foreign Policy Research Institute*, (Winter 2011): 85-113.

8. Finkelstein, David M. "China's National Military Strategy: An Overview of the "Military Strategic Guidelines" in *Right Sizing the People's Liberation Army: Exploring the Counters of China's Military*, ed. Roy Kamphausen and Andrew Scobell. Strategic Studies Institute, 2007.

9. Hodge, Homer T. "North Korea's Military Strategy." *Parameters.*

Spring 2003.

10. Hughes, Christopher W. "Japan's Military Modernization: A Quiet Japan-China Arms Race and Global Projection." *The University of Warwick.* 2009.

11. Indonesia's Defence White Paper 2008. BukuPutihPertahanan Indonesia 2008.*Indonesia's Ministry of Defence*. 2008. 60-64.

12. McDevitt, Michael. "Asian Military Modernization: Key Areas of Concern" article prepared for the conference Asia's Strategic Challenges: In Search of a Common Agenda. June, 5 2008.

Session-III

Panel-2

Second Paper

Dr. Elichi Kathara

The New Strategic Context

Despite the Korean War, the Vietnam War, and internal conflicts in Cambodia, East Timor and some other areas, we have managed the peace and stability in the Asia Pacific Region in broad terms. The Asia Pacific Region has enjoyed remarkable economic prosperity and democracy in many countries. The peace and stability has been underwritten by US strategic primacy and its alliance relations, including the US-Japan alliance which ensures US military presence in the region, thus contributing peace, stability and economic prosperity of the Asia-Pacific-Region.

Indeed, the history of the Japan-US alliance has been a great success story not just in the modern history of Japan but in the broader international history of the Asia-Pacific-Region. With the economically strong and politically stable Japan robustly allied with the United States, no country felt threatened by Japan, thus allowing East Asian countries, including China, to devote their energies to economic and social development, without feeling the need to answer a Japanese defence build-up.

Having said this, since the end of the Cold War, the strategic environment has changed significantly, and is further changing rapidly.

First, the prospect of a nuclear-armed and dictatorial North Korea with ballistic missiles would pose direct military threat to Japan and the region. It would seriously destabilize the regional balance of power. It would also test the validity of multilateral diplomacy centred on the Six-party Talks, and the credibility of the Japan-US alliance. International efforts in pursuing de-nuclearization of the Korean Peninsula have not shown any positive results. Indeed, the situation seems to be deteriorating since North Korean submarine's alleged torpedo attack on the ROK's warship Cheonan on 26 March 2010, claiming 46 lives of Korean sailors and Pyongyang's shelling of Yeonpyeong island on 23 November 2010. Despite new leader Kim Jong Un's flamboyant performance and some talks about economic reforms, the fact remains that there has been no significant change in substance of its Songun (military-first) politics and its belligerent and unpredictable external behaviour. Put simply, Pyongyang still remains determined to accelerate its nuclear and ballistic missile programme. Multilateral diplomacy of the Six-party Talks perhaps can augment an effective dissuasion strategy before Pyongyang succeeds in developing and deploying intermediate or even intercontinental ballistic missiles loaded with nuclear weapons.

The re-rise of China as a global actor presents a long-term and far-reaching challenge especially for policymakers in the region, including the Chinese themselves, given the on-going power shift driven by China's growing comprehensive national power and influence not only in the region but in the world at large, including space and cyberspace. China's increasing military spending, its relentless build-up of air and space power, submarine capability, ballistic missiles, anti-satellite, cyber-warfare capabilities and nuclear forces have aroused serious concerns throughout the countries of East Asia.

Yet China has progressively integrated into a multi-layered system of regional and global institutions, including APEC, ARF and the World Trade Organization (WTO). In particular, China has been keen to deepen economic and political cooperation with neighbouring countries, and it is clear that China's approach to Taiwan has become significantly less belligerent since Ma Ying-jeou and his Kuomintang (KMT) returned to power in 2008. Managing the growing Chinese power and influence and shaping China's strategic posture and policies would be critical if a new security order in the region is to be shaped. Indeed this represents one of the greatest challenges facing Japan and the region at large. China has become a central economic and political player not only in the region but in the global arena presents profound strategic and possibly game-changing implications for a new international order in the 21st Century world.

The situation in Afghanistan and Pakistan presents a difficult and worrisome challenge not only for America and its allied partners, but also for the international community at large, given the dangers that may arise due to acquisition of nuclear weapons by international terrorist groups thus posing a serious threat to the world. Al Qaeda and its extremist allies are still operating actively in an increasingly unstable Pakistan which is armed with more than 110 nuclear weapons. The United States, along with the international community, have so far failed to build good governance in Afghanistan and Pakistan.

There are a host of non-traditional security challenges facing the world, including cyber security, climate change, nuclear proliferation, international terrorism, energy problems, natural disasters, piracy and problems associated with failed states. It should also be noted that major powers in the region face the challenges arising from leadership transition and financial constraints. Russia had a presidential election this year. The US, China, Korea and possibly Japan will choose a new leader by the end of this year. We are very concerned about financial constraints. We expect that US defence budget will be cut in the next several years. Japan's defence budget has been decreasing for the last nine consecutive years, despite the deteriorating security environment surrounding Japan.

Japan's Strategic Policy

I argue that given the power shift that has been underway in the region with rising China and India and US hegemonic decline, the time has come for Japan to rethink its post-war strategic policy and think through its strategic options for the future.

The new National Defence Program Guidelines (2010 NDPG) adopted on 17 December 2010, is a policy document that approximates the defence strategy of the Japanese government for the next ten years, which lays out security objectives and means of Japan's defence policy and its force structure. The fundamentals of Japan's security policy such as the exclusively defensive defence policy and the three non-nuclear principles remain intact, yet there are six notable features in the new NDPG reflecting Tokyo's changing perceptions of the strategic environment and new defence requirements. First, the NDPG calls for "a body at the Prime Minister's Office dedicated to security policy coordination among relevant ministers and advice to the Prime Minister," perhaps Japan's equivalent of

US National Security Council (NSC). Second, the time-honoured concept of the "Basic Defence Force Concept" – a concept focused on static existence of defence capability so as to prevent a security vacuum arising - is superseded by "Dynamic Defence Force," a new concept which aims to enhance "the credibility of Japan's deterrent capability by promoting timely and active 'operations.' It should be noted, however, that Dynamic Defence Force cannot be interpreted as involving offensive, counter-force strike capability; the emphasis of Dynamic Defence Force is placed on readiness, mobility and flexibility and seamless operations of intelligence, surveillance and reconnaissance (ISR) capabilities. Third, the new document calls for further strengthening the Japan-US alliance in a wide array of policy areas including a continuous review of common strategic objectives and roles, missions and capabilities, missile defence, strategic dialogue aimed at improving credibility of extended deterrence, maritime security, peace cooperation activities, and cyber space security. Fourth, with regard to force structure there has been a shift in focus to the security of remote southwest islands. Hence, the Mid Term Defence Plan (FY 2011-2015), which was announced along with the NDPG, calls for deployment of new units in island areas of southwest Japan. Finally, the NDPG highlights the importance of promoting multi-layered security cooperation, including promotion of security cooperation with several like-minded countries such as the ROK, Australia, ASEAN and India.

Building Blocks for Regional Security Architecture

Professor Hedley Bull argued in his classic study *The Anarchical Society*, there are five contextual factors that can provide or contribute to international order. The first is a favourable balance of power meaning that "a state of affairs such that no one power is in a position where it is preponderant and can lay down the law to others". The second is international law. The third is diplomacy. The fourth is the role of great powers. And the fifth is war. In some cases where order is broken, we may resort to war as in the case of the 1991 Persian Gulf War.

'Security architecture' can be considered as yet another useful construct that can provide or contribute to international order. More specifically, security architecture can play a critical role in meeting traditional security challenges in the region (the Korean Peninsula, Taiwan, territorial disputes) through dialogues, confidence building measures, deterrence and contingency planning, crisis and conflict management, escalation control, and resolution of conflict. Security architecture can also play an important role in meeting non-traditional security challenges (climate change, natural disasters, terrorism, epidemics, etc.) through dialogue, confidence building measures, capacity building, joint training and exercises.

There are three strands of security architecture discernible in the Asia-Pacific-Region. The first strand consists of the United States and its alliances and partnerships, including America's alliances with Japan, South Korea, and Australia. The United States has been strengthening not only its traditional "hub and spoke" system of alliances founded on bilateral framework, but also "mini-lateral" relations such as US-Japan-India, US-Japan-South Korea, and US-Japan-Australia.

From the year 2011 onwards, the Obama Administration has been pursuing "rebalancing" strategy toward the Asia Pacific region in an effort to strengthen US credibility in the region in an age of fiscal austerity. During 2011 Washington pushed forward strengthening its security cooperation with Singapore, the Philippines, Vietnam, and Indonesia. It announced new deployments or rotations of troops and equipment to Singapore and Australia. It should also be noted that the coastal areas of South Asia and the Indian Ocean are now included in the US Administration's regional strategy.

Notwithstanding, there are three problems. First, US rebalancing strategy can be interpreted by China as containment and/or encirclement, thus causing security dilemma and US-China strategic competition or possibly confrontation. Second, it would be difficult to gain public support in the region due to divergent perceptions, deepening economic ties with China and the risks of war. Third, given fiscal conditions and budgetary constraints in the US, Japan and other states, the US and its allies cannot afford to increase defence budgets significantly and hence may not be able to enhance deterrent capabilities substantially.

An enduring element of US strategy in the context of maintaining credibility of security commitment concerns "extended deterrence" (both nuclear and conventional) and missile defence architecture. Yet the US efforts on this front would be perceived by China as threatening and requiring Chinese response.

The second strand of security architecture concerns stable US-China relations. The Obama Administration has been seeking to establish "positive, cooperative and comprehensive US-China partnership." In this context, Washington initiated the Strategic Security Dialogue talks that parallel the Strategic and Economic Dialogue, while maintaining military-to-military relations including Military Maritime Consultative Agreement (MMCA).

The third strand of security architecture consists of a wide variety of multi-lateral institutions and mechanisms. They include the flowing:

- ASEAN-led institutions: EAS, ARF, ASEAN+3, ADMM Plus.

- South Asian Association for Regional Cooperation (SAARC).

- Shanghai Cooperation Organization (SCO).

- Six-Party Talks on North Korean nuclear issues.

- Joint military training and exercises: Pacific Partnership, Cobra Gold, Regional Cooperation Agreement on Combating Piracy and Armed Robbery against Ships in Asia (ReCAAP).

- International law and organizations: 1982 United Nations Convention on the Law of the Sea (UNCLOS); International Maritime Organization (IMO); International Court of Justice (ICJ); export control regimes, Proliferation Security Initiatives(PSI), etc.

Future Challenges Facing the Asia-Pacific-Region

We will face the choice between a concert of great powers or US-China confrontation. To avoid US-China confrontation, it would be crucial to strategically and proactively co-opt China in regional architecture building. It is widely recognized that community building efforts in the region have been driven by economic integration with ASEAN in the driver's seat. However, when it comes to a broader, region-wide architecture, it can be argued that Japan, US and China can be expected to play a more prominent role in architecture building in the region.

An idea that has been looming large on Japan's policy agenda is of a US-Japan-China trilateral mechanism for comprehensive strategic dialogues and consultations at the official level on wide-ranging security issues encompassing maritime security, international terrorism, the proliferation of WMD, international peace-keeping, and a host of "human security issues," including climate change, pandemics and natural disasters. A US-Japan-China trilateral mechanism could also involve trilateral measures for cooperation in the fields of defence exchanges, military training and exercises. In times of international crises, such as incidents in the maritime domain, there would be hot-line channels of communication among the defence establishments of the three countries so that they could coordinate policy measures in timely and effective ways.

It would also be important for the countries in the region to develop common norms, rules of the game, crisis management mechanisms, revitalizing, promoting maritime communication mechanisms between Japan and China the U.S-China MMCA and establishing Code of Conduct in the South China Sea.

Major and middle powers in the region should promote "capacity building" measures bilaterally or under the aegis of the ADMM Plus. The Experts' Working Groups set up by the ADMM Plus which are currently engaged in five areas -HA/DR, maritime security, terrorism, military medicine, and Peace Keeping Operations (PKO) would provide a unique opportunity for deepening and widening security cooperation.

Finally, traditional security issues and concerns need to be addressed. They include the tension on the Korean peninsula, the Taiwan problem, maritime security issues, and the diplomatic or territorial issues. In this connection, let me make some personal observations on the Senkaku issue. The Senkaku Issue has been a diplomatic issue, if not a territorial issue between Japan and China that has plagued Japan's relations with China. In my view, the circumstances deteriorated partly due to misjudgment and mismanagement on the part of the government of Japan and partly due to changing power relationship between Japan and China. The Japanese government's recent decision to 'nationalize' the islands via purchasing three of the islands from a private owner was perceived by Beijing as an outright action to change the status quo, an action that could solidify Japan's control of the islands. The GOJ feared that a purchase by Tokyo Metropolitan government, which was initiated and promoted by its governor Shin taro Ishihara, would destabilize the situation possibly leading to loss of the central government control of the islands. The government of Japan apparently hoped that defying Chinese objections arising not only from the Chinese Foreign Ministry but also from almost every member of the Chinese Communist Party's Politburo standing committee would make the unpopular DPJ government look tough in the face of Chinese pressures, without seriously considering the consequence of its behaviour. One could be forgiven for saying that Japan's cabinet decision to nationalize three of the Senkaku islands unnecessarily provoked Chinese nationalism at a time when China was entering a critical period of leadership transition.

To manage the Japan-China relationship, three things are of paramount importance. First, Japan and China must maintain a good sense of proportion when making foreign policy decisions. Japan-China relations must be based upon mutually beneficial strategic interests, not nationalistic sentiment or politicians' opportunism. Second, despite some ups and downs in the relationship, both governments should keep negotiation channels open and continue practical policy matters at the working level. Third, both governments should avoid unnecessarily provocative statements or behaviour and try to manage rising nationalism on both sides.

In tackling a host of difficult challenges, traditional and non-traditional, the starting point is that we should know each other, learn from each other and understand each other's intentions and capabilities. And this requires a lot of work. This is actually one of the lessons Japan learned from the 11 March 2011 triple disaster- the earthquake, tsunami and nuclear accident. When Japan and the United States tried to cope with the grave nuclear accident in Fukushima both Tokyo and Washington initially did not know each other's capabilities enough. Nor were they seeing eye-to-eye with regard to each other's objectives in responding to the accident. Unlike *Operation Tomodachi* where the Japanese Self-Defence Forces, and US forces carried out a joint operation successfully, the quality of communication (especially information sharing) between Japan's and America's nuclear authorities and parties concerned in the initial phase of the accident was less than optimal in face of a critical situation. Fukushima was indicative of the kind of communication gap that Japan and the US still need to bridge to strengthen the bilateral relationship.

Let me conclude by saying that at this critical juncture we need to get back to the basics: we should begin by knowing each other and understanding each other better, while grasping the larger strategic context.

Session-III

Panel-2

Third Paper

Major General BK Sharma, AVSM, SM**(Retd)

Asia-Pacific: Future Security Challenges and Opportunities

General

Secretary of state, Hillary Clinton in her speech titled America's Pacific Century delivered in Hawaii in Nov 2011, described the Asia –Pacific region as, "Stretching from the Indian sub- continent to the western shores of America, the region spans two oceans-the Pacific and the Indian that are increasingly linked by shipping and strategy". General XiongGuangaki, former Deputy Chief of General staff and Chairman of China Institute of International Strategic Studies at the 3rd meeting of the 2nd Track High Level Dialogue on Sino – US relations, remarked that Clinton's definition of the region is coloured by the area of responsibility of the US Pacific Command. He argued that Asia –Pacific generally refers to the region that is best represented by APEC, comprising 21 member countries of the Pacific Rim region. Other strategic analysts term Asia-Pacific as a system of systems, consisting of the traditional East Asian, Southeast Asian and Asia-Pacific sub systems. The South Asian sub-system, though geographically segregated, is integrated because of common maritime security dynamics, trade linkages and non-traditional threats. Therefore, from a broad strategic perspective, Indian Ocean Region (IOR) and Western Pacific connected through South China Sea (SCS) form a common strategic space for power shifts of the 21st century.

Geostrategic importance

The region encompasses almost half of world population, three of ten largest economies, more than fifth of world GDP, 1/3 of world exports and half of the world's maritime tonnage. It is estimated that even at a conservative growth rate of about 6.5%, China, India and South East Asian states will be the engines of world economic growth. The region is the maritime trade highway of the world. It joins South East Asian states with Western Pacific, functioning as the throat of sea routes punctuated by Strait of Malacca, Sunda, Lambok and Makassar. Roughly two-thirds of South Korea's energy supplies, nearly 60 per cent of Japan's and Taiwan's energy supplies, and about 70 per cent of China's crude-oil imports come through SCS. East China Sea (ECS) and SCS are rich in fisheries and provide an important source of protein for millions of people, while the seabed is reputed to hold valuable reserves of energy deposits. As for IOR, China imports more than 60 per cent its oil from the Middle East and its dependence is estimated to exceed the 65 per cent mark by 2030. Uninterrupted flow of oil, natural resources and goods is extremely crucial for developing economies, like India and China.

Security Scenario

During the Cold War the security architecture in Asia-Pacific was based on military alliances. However, in the post- Cold War era security encompasses commerce and trade, energy, territorial disputes, proliferation of weapons of mass destruction, cyber warfare, piracy, Jihadi organizations (Abu Sayyaf Group, Jemaah Islamiyah, Moro Islamic Liberation Front), environment (tsunamis, earthquakes, nuclear disasters) and a host of Non-Traditional Military Threats (NTMT). The focus of this paper is on East and Southeast Asia. The major issue that mires the regional security prospects is of contested sovereignty and maritime boundary claims among China, Taiwan, Vietnam, Philippines, Malaysia and Brunei over a host of small islands, reefs and their adjacent waters. China claims 80% of SCS based on a 'Nine Dotted Claim-line' which was drawn by KMT in 1947, and adopted by PRC in 1953. However, other littoral states stake their respective ownerships over the island territories, based on traditional fishing activities, inheritance from the colonial past and the UNCLOS treaty of 1982.

Since 2007, tensions in the region have escalated due to continued demand for energy resources, rising nationalism, disputes over fishing grounds, advances in military capabilities, and attempts by the various claimants to bolster their sovereignty claims through domestic legislations, the establishment of administrative bodies and submission to international regimes. The stand offs between Chinese vessels and US naval ships, with fishing boats and energy vessels of Philippines and Vietnam, and the recent Scarborough Shoal and Senkaku / Diayau incidents, point to growing potential of conflict in the region. The South Korea-Japan dispute over DokdoTakeshima is another matter of concern.

Dynamics of Strategic Competition

US

Hillary Clinton articulates the importance of Asia-Pacific in these words, "In the next 10 years , we need to be smart and systematic about where we invest time and energy, so that we put ourselves in the best position to sustain our leadership, secure our interests and advance our values. One of the most important tasks of American statecraft over the next decade will, therefore, be to lock in a substantially increased investment-diplomatic, economic, strategic, and otherwise-in the Asia- Pacific region." She underscores investments by American companies, freedom of navigation in the SCS, countering proliferation efforts of North Korea, and ensuring the transparency in the military activities of the region's key players as the main strategic objectives. The enunciated strategy is marked by six guidelines; strengthening bilateral security alliances, deepening relationship with emerging powers, including with China and Vietnam; engaging with multilateral institutions, expanding trade and investment, forging a broad-based military presence, and advancing democracy and human rights. Treaty alliances with Japan, South Korea, Australia, the Philippines and Thailand are noted as the fulcrum of strategic turn to the Asia–Pacific.

The central pillar of this policy is manifest in its recently declared Asia Pivot / Rebalancing Strategy. These strategies are purportedly aimed at countervailing China and deterring Iran. As part of this strategy, the US plans to deploy 60% of its naval assets in the Western Pacific and Indian Ocean and may secure military bases in Subic Bay, Clark Air Base (Philippines), Okinawa (Japan), and Darwin (Australia) besides deployments in Indonesia, Singapore and Thailand. The US may evince interest in

CamRanh Port (Vietnam). The US – Australia joint defense arrangement facilitates intelligence collection, ballistic missile early warning, submarine communication and satellite based communication. Besides, US – New Zealand defense cooperation is likely to witness major upgrade; the latter being a major 'Non NATO Ally' of the US.

The US 'Hub and Spoke',military strategy envisages using GUAM in the Pacific Ocean and Diego Garcia in the Indian Ocean as the two hubs, and the operating bases in rim of two oceans as spokes. The sword arms of this strategy are Carrier Battle Groups and attack submarines which can be deployed to choke the strategic straits in Indian Ocean, Strait of Malacca, Strait of Makassar etc.

On the economic front, forging of Trans Pacific Partnership (TPP), which excludes China, appears as the principal objective. The US politico-diplomatic, economic and military activism is seen by China as an attempt designed at Grand Encirclement being knit by the US and its proxies in the region. The Asia Pivot strategy, therefore,carriesattendant risks of provoking China, and militarizing the region.

China

China on the other hand, emboldened by its economic growth, continues with its ambitious military modernization programme, thus adding teeth to its 'Counter Intervention Strategy'. As per a forecast carried in the Economist publication titled, "20 MEGACHANGE 50: The World in 2050", by 2040 China's economy would have surpassed that of US .The forecast is based on the assessments of Asian Development Bank (ADB), Carnegie Endowment for International Peace, Goldman Sachs and Pricewaterhouse Cooper, As per Goldman Sachs projections, if US economy grows at 2 per cent and China's at 6per cent, China will overtake the US by 2027. It is estimated that China will be able to afford about 2 per cent of its GDP for defence, which would be approximately 200 billion US dollars. As per SIPRI, by the year 2035, if China's economic growth continues, its defence spending will surpass that of the US.

China considers Western Pacific vital for its sovereignty, integrity, security and development. The 2008 Defense White paper, highlights the importance of "struggle for strategic resources, strategic locations and strategic dominance". For geographically restrained China, the security of coastal economic centers of gravity, access to energy, raw materials, export markets and security of SLOCs are critical.78 % of oil to PRC is transported by the Western SLOCs, passing through maritime choke points of Southeast Asia (i.e the Malacca, Sunda, and Lombok-Makassar straits). The PLAN's counter–piracy missions in the Gulf of Aden and its much debated 'Malacca Dilemma' underscore the seriousness of Beijing's security concerns along this route. Therefore, in China's security calculus, SCS assumes great strategic importance. In 2006, president Hu Jintao described the PRC as 'a great maritime power' and urged the transformation of navy from 'near seas active defense' (first group of islands i.e. Kurlie, Taiwan, SCS) to 'far sea defense' (second group of islands from Japan , GUAM, northwest Pacific ocean and even the Indian Ocean).

Taiwan is the fulcrum of China's maritime security; it was rightly termed by McArthur as an 'Unsinkable Aircraft Carrier'. Military logic reveals that occupation of Taiwan by a hostile regime or military power and blocking of SCS and ECS, can cause China's perceived economic strangulation. China's policy of graduated assimilation of Taiwan seems to be working well. The Economic Cooperation Framework Agreement – 2010, has given a boost to commerce and trade and people to people contact,thus minimizing chances of a military conflict over the Taiwan issue.

China pursued a decade of soft power economic engagement policy with South East Asian countries under the aegis of East Asia Summit, Greater Mekong Sub Region Initiative (Cambodia, Laos, Myanmar, Thailand and Yunnan Province of China), leading to its emergence as the largest trading partner of Southeast Asia, with combined trade exceeding US$ 200 billion. However, divergent claims on island territories and EEZ by the rim-land countries, have led to tensions and military assertion by the protagonists. China has strengthened its military presence at Sanya on Hainan Island and SanshaPrefecture on Woody Island, and demonstrated military assertion at Reed Bank, Mischeef Reef, Senkaku/ Diaoyu islands, oil blocks in Spratly Islands etc.The other contestants too have asserted their claimed sovereignty.

China's approach to military transformation is based on 'RMA with Chinese Characteristics', with focus on development of 'Pockets of Excellence' forces and Acupuncture/Paralysis warfare. China's asymmetric warfare capability has achieved a moderate level of sophistication. China's hi-tech enabled navy & air force, offensive cyber warfare capability, anti-satellite weapons, assured second strike nuclear capability and 'Assassin's Mace' weapons have lent credibility to its 'Anti- Access Anti- Denial' (A2-AD) strategy against US led intervention forces. China considers the export of strategic products, development of infrastructure and economic aid as viable leverages to protect its national interests. The territorial disputes and consequent military assertion posea most serious challenge to regional security, with potential to draw the US into the conflict. The critical uncertainty, which merits a watch, is howwill China allay the concerns of East Asian states, so that they do not take recourse to any anti-China strategic or military alliances?

Japan

Japan appears to have reset its earlier policy of 'Reduced Reliance on US and Politico-Economic Engagement with China' to one which seeks enhanced security ties with the US. China's military assertion, threat to SLOCs, nuclear threat from North Korea and the 'Kurile Island Chain Issue' with Russia, mark the reason for this shift. Japan's Defence Policy Programme - 2012, underscores the need for a dynamic transformation of its Defence Forces, from basic defence to offensive defense capability, to protect its off shore island territories. Japan seeks to deploy a two layered 'ABM system' (AEGIS Destroyers / PAC-3 Patriot Missile). Japan has proposed a new initiative termed as 'Rim-land Security', in concert with India, South East Asia littorals, South Korea,Australia and New Zealand. The issue of the so called purchase of Senkaku Islands in Sep 2012, has led to sporadic stand offs at sea, and public demonstrations in both the countries. Sovereignty over Senkaku islands has become a symbol of national pride and apotential flash point.

Koreas

Recent incidents like a North Korean submarine allegedly sinking a South Korea Ship (Chenon) and shelling its island (Yeonpyeong), and conduct of nuclear tests by North Korea, perpetuate security concerns of South Korea and Japan. South Korea, too, seeks to deploy the Anti-Missile Radar Shield (Aegis KDX III) against short range missile barrages, as part of the BMD Shield (PAC -2 AD), reportedly woven with US help.

Dire economic situation in North Korea can potentially create internal unrest and pose a challenge of humanitarian security. Any such development will have serious security ramifications, if US and China take divergently opposite positions.Unification of Korea, if it occurs, will be a game changer and alter the geopolitical landscape of the region with serious security ramifications.

Vietnam

Vietnam asserts its sovereignty over the Paracel and Spratly Islands, based on the activities of Vietnamese fishermen, inheritance from former colonial power France and the occupation and administration of 21 islets in the Spratlys (the largest number occupied by any of the disputants). In 1974, PLA had evicted South Vietnamese forces from Paracels and in 1998 from Johnson Reef at Spratlys. A Chinese legislation, in 2007, that designated the islands under the administration of Hainan Island, had drawn unprecedented anti-China demonstrations in Vietnam. The tension arose in 2011, when the Chinese patrol vessels reportedly cut the cables of survey ships near contested oil blocks in Spratly islands. Vietnam's defense paper laments, "Complicated developments in SCS have negatively affected maritime economic development of Vietnam. It has strengthened its defences at atolls under its occupation, is spending more money on its defence forces and is seeking closer ties with US, India and Japan.

The Philippines

Since 1995, when PLA occupied and built structures on Mischeef Reef, there have been series of stand offs between Chinese and Philippines naval forces in the Spratlys. Upswing in economic relations or measures to undertake joint seismic surveys in the disputed waters did not lead to any substantial improvement in bilateral relations. The passage of legislation in the Philippines, to update the country's archipelagic baseline claims and Manila's subsequent submission to the CLCS in 2009, strained relations further. Recently, the Scarborough shoal incident has caused serious tension between the two countries. Philippineslacksthe military capability to pursue its claims in SCS. It seeks US help to enhance its defence preparedness under the aegis of 'Most Favoured Non NATO Ally'.

ASEAN

For decades ASEAN has gently sought to bring coherence to a region of enormous political and economic differences. However, emerging strategic competition in the region is somewhat widening the division in the ten-member grouping over China's maritime claims in SCS. Members with claims in SCS, supported by Singapore and Thailand, want ASEAN to register concerns over China's perceived belligerent actions. However, non-claimants, mainly Cambodia supported by Laos and Myanmar, tend to go along with China's insistence on dealing with the issue bilaterally. China, as one writer puts it, may have obtained an 'outsider's veto' over ASEAN, when its interests are threatened. The Philippines and Vietnam look openly to America for military and diplomatic support. Thailand and the Philippines are treaty allies of America, which is also revving up its military engagement with Singapore. The remainder of ASEAN, however,is against the militarization of the region. ASEAN favours institutionalization of Declaration of Conduct (DoC) of Parties ,implementation of Code of Conduct (CoC) and creation of 'Regional Comprehensive Economic Partnership'(RCEP) for the economic integration of the region'.

Russia

Russia accords greater importance to its 'Far Eastern Policy' in terms of energy exports, container trade and access to export markets for its goods. Melting of the Arctic, is expected to open far reaching strategic opportunities for Russia, providing it access to untold mineral wealth and drastically shorter shipping routes to the Atlantic. The US Geological Survey has estimated that some 30% of the world's undiscovered oil lies in the Arctic. It also contains coal, iron, uranium, gold, copper, rare earths, gem stones and fish. Due to melting of ice North-East Passage above Russia, also known as the Northern Sea Route (NSR), have become partially navigable several months each summer. Russian ships are known to venture on NSR. China's Yue Long (Snow Dragon), the world's largest non-nuclear-powered ice breaker and some other ships, are known to traverse NSR. China is strongly lobbying for permanent observer status on the Arctic council (America, Canada, Denmark, Norway and Russia). Russian scholars argue, "Whoever has control over the Arctic route will control the new passage of world economics and international strategies". This argument is premised on the basis of a survey that most of the Arctic region will fall within the 200 miles of Exclusive Economic Zone (EEZ) of Russia, as per UNCLOS. Russia is increasingly conscious of emergence of NSR, passing through the Arctic region, as an alternate to Western SLOCS, and would leverage its geostrategic position to stake claims on natural resources and rightsof passage.

India

India's Look East Policy seeks inter-alia engagement of East Asia and the Pacific Region. In the words of Dr Manmohan Singh, "India's Look East Policy is not merely an external economic policy; it also marks a strategic shift in India's vision of the world and its place in the evolving global economy. Most of all, it is reaching out to our civilization neighbours in Southeast Asia and East Asia".India supports the creation of a Pan-Asian Free Trade Area (FTA), comprehensive economic cooperation, and collective security of SLOCs, critical infrastructure, cyberspace and collaborative measures against NTMT. India strongly advocates bilateral and amicable resolution of inter-state disputes and a sound climate change strategy. Engagement with China, and a close strategic relationship with the US and other countries, will remain the cornerstones of its 'Look East Policy'. India seeks a free and just world order, wherein among other things, it has access to global common resources and markets, and freedom of navigation in the international waters.

Towards a Collaborative Regional Framework

Presently, Asia- Pacific Regional Framework initiatives include organizations such as APEC, which places stress on economic cooperation, ASEAN Regional Forum (ARF) which focuses on security cooperation and East Asia Summit, which is multi-disciplinary in its construct. There is a need to energize the functioning of these organizations and use these platforms for constructive dialogue and building trust. The emerging organizations, such as TPP and Regional Comprehensive Economic Partnership, should work towards building economic interdependence. China and the US should work more closely on the issue of North Korea, under the aegis of Six – Party Talks for a nuclear-free Korean peninsula. The regional countries should seriously work on the promulgation of the Declaration of Conduct (DoC) of Parties in SCS, duly supported by the UN. Confidence building measures should include the following:-

- Expand the scope of Paragraph 5 of DoC to include freeze on up gradation of military structures in the disputed areas.

- Revamp the mechanism of conducting annual defence and security dialogues between ASEAN and China.

- Establish Joint Working Group (JWG) to discuss:

  - Notification of planned military exercises to each other, clearly spelling out, aim, objectives and force levels.

  - Establish hotlines between the defence ministries of claimant countries to report and manage untoward incidents.

  - Sign agreements on prevention of incidents at sea, between the claimants.

  - Create regional cooperation framework agreements for combating piracy, terrorism, conducting joint naval patrolling and search and rescue operations.

  - Evolve a cooperative mechanism for coordinated assistance for humanitarian security in the event of natural disasters.

  - Build in more transparency in military modernization programmes by publishing White Papers and free and frank dialogue at the ASEAN Regional Forum (ARF)/ Shangri-La Dialogue and the forum of ASEAN Defence Ministers Meeting Plus (ADDM- Plus).

Concluding Remarks

A disturbed security environment in Asia- Pacific will adversely affect, flow of energy, commerce and trade, leading to escalation of oil prices and hurting global economy. In the larger interest of humanity, it is imperative that every stakeholder acts responsibly and contributes towards the resolution of disputes. Time is critical, and we must act in right earnest to build confidence and create frameworks for enduring peace and stability in the region.

Session-III

Panel-2

Fourth Paper

Dr. Tuan Yao Cheng

Disputes of Diaoyutai/Senkaku Islands

The recent clashes over the Diaoyutai/ Senkaku Islands between Japan, mainland China and Taiwan have been the most explosive conflicts in the East China Sea for the last three decades. Not only it undermines the peaceful relations of the three countries but also it might pose a great challenge to regional security, if it is not properly managed. Though the clashes are now winding down to a less provocative extent, the disputes remain unchanged and they might escalate any time.

The disputed islands, called the Diaoyutai Islands in Taiwan, Senkaku Islands in Japan and Diaoyu Islands in China, that lie 100 nautical miles northeast of Taiwan, are claimed as the national territory by Taiwan, mainland China and Japan. At the end of World War II in 1945, the islands were under the US control as part of the captured Japanese island of Okinawa but have been under Japan's administrative jurisdiction since 1972 when Okinawa was returned to Japan. Both Taiwan and mainland China disputed the handover of control of the islands to Japan and asserted their sovereignty claims since then.

The recent controversies erupted due to Japan's domestic politics. In early this year, the Governor of Tokyo Ishihara Shin taro proposed to purchase the islands with private funds and planned to build shelters for Japanese vessels. In order to restrain the reckless act of Shin taro and serve "peaceful and stable maintenance of the islands," the Noda government decided to nationalize the islands. It was also motivated by political gain in the upcoming election, a move supported by many in Japan. The Japanese government officially signed a deal in September 12 to purchase from a private Japanese family recognized as the owner with the payment of ¥ 2.05 billion.

Considering the act of nationalization highly politicized, provocative and illegal, both Taiwan and mainland China made strong protests and did not recognize any unilateral action taken by Japan to nationalize the islands. Taiwan Foreign Minister Timothy Yang responded, "We lodged a severe protest over Tokyo's so-called move to nationalize the Diaoyutai Islands, which has seriously infringed on Taiwan's sovereignty, jeopardized bilateral ties and escalated regional conflicts. We strongly demand Japan to immediately stop all action to undermine Taiwan's territorial sovereignty and revoke its illegal purchase of the islets." The Chinese Foreign Ministry was quick to blast the nationalization and said, "This is a serious infringement of China's sovereignty and has seriously hurt the feelings of 1.3 billion Chinese. The Chinese government and people express their resolute opposition and protest strongly." Moreover, immediately after Japanese purchase, China sent surveillance and patrol ships to waters surrounding the islands to reassert its claim.

East China Sea Peace Initiative

Prior to Japan's nationalization of the islands, President Ma proposed a peace initiative on 5 August 2012 to address territorial disputes over the Diaoyutai Islands. At the ceremony of commemorating the 60th anniversary of the Sino-Japanese peace treaty, Ma reassured the cooperative relationship between Taiwan and Japan that "the friendship is at a level unprecedented in the last 40 years;" however, he was also worried about the tensions associated with the dispute over the Diaoyutai Islands. Raising concerns about the disputes which could lead to uncertainties and disrupt regional peace and security, he proposed an "East China Sea Peace Initiative" by which he urged all parties concerned to: (1) Refrain from taking any antagonistic actions. (2) Shelve controversies. (3) Observe international law and resolve disputes through peaceful means. (4) Seek consensus on a code of conduct in East China Sea. (5) Establish a mechanism for cooperation on exploring and developing resources in the East China Sea.

He also noted that there was a need to face the problem and recognize the existence of the dispute of the islands. He called for putting aside differences and developing resources since natural resources could be shared with each other. Furthermore, he reminded the concerned parties in the region that the region had gone through hardship to achieve high economic development. No one would like to see Northeast Asia ever again succumb to the catastrophe of war.

Again on 7 September 2012, Ma made a visit to Pengjia Islet, the part of Taiwan closest to the Diaoyutai Islands, and released the implementation guidelines for the peace initiative. The guidelines suggest a two-stage approach, peaceful dialogues and cooperative exploration and development of resources. In the first stage, the concerned parties could start by holding three separate bilateral dialogues – between Taiwan and Japan, between Taiwan and mainland China, and between Japan and the mainland. Once they reach agreements, they could gradually move towards a single trilateral negotiation process. In the second stage, it involves institutionalizing all forms of dialogue and negotiation, and establishes mechanism for joint exploration and development of resources. As Ma emphasized, "if all parties concerned could agree to set aside the sovereignty issues and explore the feasibility of joint exploration in the spirit of peaceful cooperation, then we could gradually attain the goal of sharing resources."

There were also a number of points noted by Ma regarding implementing the guidelines. First, the peace initiative is not new; it has been successfully practiced by other countries. For example, Europe experienced sovereignty dispute in the North Sea; however, through negotiations on joint development and sharing of oil resources, the countries have successfully transformed Brent Crude into a world-renewed brand. Second, there exists some kind of agreement or negotiations among the three countries. For instance, Taiwan has been negotiating with Japan on a fishery agreement for a long period of time, it also engages with mainland China on oil and gas exploration in the Taiwan Strait; and China and Japan have fishing and petroleum agreements. Yet, the existing mechanisms for mutual interaction and cooperation have not gone smoothly, so the proposed initiative might be helpful to tune up the process. Third, the formats of dialogue or negotiations could be rather flexible, whether to adopt by track I or track II. It seems that Ma understands quite well the absence of diplomatic relations between Taiwan and Japan, and the special relationships between the two sides across the Taiwan Strait. And fourth, there are many issues for the concerned parties to negotiate with, including fishing, mining, marine science research, marine environmental protection, maritime security, and unconventional security. Hence, as long as the parties concerned agree to shelve the sovereignty issue, they could start to explore common interests.

Taiwan's Protest Activities

After Japan nationalized the Diaoyutai Islands, China launched a series of large-scale protest activities, including sending Chinese marine surveillance vessels to the areas of the islands, massive anti-Japanese demonstrations in numerous Chinese cities, and call for boycott of Japanese goods in China. As compared to China, Taiwan has been more moderate and restrained. At least no large-scale anti-Japanese demonstrations have occurred and the bilateral economic relations are not affected by the island dispute.

Despite restrained reactions, many people are upset with Japan's nationalization of the islands. On 23 September 2012, hundreds of people took to the street to protest against Japan. The protesters chanted "Protecting Diaoyutai, Diaoyutai are ours." Some of them urged the Taiwan government to get tougher on the Diaoyutai issue and take concrete action. The protest event was organized by several local civil groups, joined by a number of lawmakers of the Kuomintang Party (KMT), the ruling party, but without the presence of the lawmakers of the Democratic Progressive Party (DPP), the opposition party. The DPP is pro-Taiwan independence and does not want to team up with China on the issue of the Diaoyutai Islands.

Two days later, on 25 September 2012, Taiwan fishermen launched a large-scale protest against Japan and asserted their rights to operate in the waters of the Diaoyutai islands, claimed as their traditional fishing grounds. About 75 Taiwanese fishing boats, escorted by 10 Coast Guard Administration (CGA) ships, embarked on a protest voyage to the Diaoyutai. They sailed as close as 3 nautical miles to the islands and were held back by Japanese coast guard vessels by flashlights and water cannons. Taiwan's CGA ships responded by firing water cannons and shouting protests using loudspeakers. Unable to move forward and considering the rough sea conditions, the fishing boats ended demonstration and returned to port. They were given a hero's welcome when they came back to Taiwan.

On 10 October 2012, the national day of the Republic of China (Taiwan), Taiwan government displayed advertisement in four major US newspapers, the Los Angeles Times, New York Times, Wall street Journal, and Washington Post. It highlighted Taiwan's sovereignty over the Diaoyutai Islands and called for resolution of the dispute by the proposed East China Sea Peace Initiative.

Japan's Response

Japan's response to Ma's peace initiative was very subtle and diplomatic, no rejection and no acceptance. Just a few days after Ma's peace proposal, Japanese Foreign Minister Koichiro Gemba said on 7 August 2012 that Japanese government cannot accept the idea expressed by Taiwan because the Senkaku Islands are Japan's integral territory. However, he stressed, this will not affect the friendly relations between Taiwan and Japan. It is helpful to promote concrete cooperation to maintain peace and stability in the East China Sea. He indicated, that Japan had no concrete proposals with regard to the type of cooperation, but there is room for brain-storming.

After Taiwan fishermen protest activities, a statement was released by Minister Gemba on 5 October 2012 through Japan's Interchange Association, which represents Japan's foreign office in Taiwan in the absence of diplomatic ties. The tone of the statement was considered more conciliatory. It is said that Japan agreed with the basic concept and spirit of Taiwan's East China Sea Peace Initiative, although some parts of the initiative and implementation guidelines were unacceptable to Japan. "Geography proximity between Taiwan and Japan may result in some 'unsettled issues,' but the important thing is that we handle such matters in a calm and rational manner through communication and not let bilateral ties be affected by 'isolated cases.'" Although the statement does not mention the Diaoyutai Islands explicitly, the unsettled issues refer to the disputes between the two countries. Some observers consider that Japan's description of the dispute over the Diaoyutai as "unsettled issues" could be seen as a concession in tone, since earlier Japan had refused to acknowledge that there was a territorial dispute over the Diaoyutai. Taiwan's Foreign Ministry spokesman responded, "This is an indication of Japan's demonstration of good will."

In addition, Japan proposed to resume bilateral fishery talks, which had been stalled since 2009 due to differences on how to resolve the cross-border fishery dispute. It is what Ma's government likes to see. In part, it was a positive response to Ma's peace initiative, interpreted by Taiwan. In part, the right of Taiwan's fishermen to fish in Diaoyutai waters has long been a friction between the two countries, and a resolution is deemed necessary. Japan, by agreeing to reopen the fishery talks was able to keep Taiwan from aligning with China in the dispute over the Senkaku Islands. And the talks are only on fishing rights instead of sovereignty issue.

China and US Response

Beijing did not give a direct response to Ma's peace initiative. It only indicated in a written statement from Chinese Ministry of Foreign Affairs that "We have noted the talks made by Taiwan's leader on August 5. All the Chinese people shall have the responsibility to defend the sovereignty of the Diaoyutai Islands and the rights of East China Sea."

Notwithstanding, there are plenty of comments and critiques from Chinese news media with regard to Ma's peace initiative. One kind of view is giving positive response to its peace approach to the dispute, considering it is constructive, rational, and a timely initiative. It is not in the interest of China to escalate the conflict with Japan over the Diaoyutai during the present period. It is better to solve the dispute through negotiations and peaceful means. Another view is that it is in China's interest to maintain peace with Japan, but it does not address the problem of unilateral change. That is, China is willing to maintain the status quo of the Diaoyutai under the current circumstances, however; no country can be allowed to make unilateral changes.

The third view is more critical of the initiative, believing that it is a smart strategy pursued by Taiwan for protecting its foreign relations interests. It dare not to confront Japan and the United States on sovereignty issues over Diaoyutai since the two countries are main supporters of Taiwan, even though it likes to voice its concerns over the issue. It is not willing to negotiate and work with China on island issue on bilateral basis but it will bring Taiwan to the international set if China agrees to join Ma's peace initiative, which includes three countries in the negotiation process. And the fourth view is rejection of Ma's initiative. It deems the initiative useless because it is not able to stop Japan's occupation of the islands by peaceful means. What Taiwan needs to do is to join China with collective action to protect Chinese territory.

In other words, Ma's peace initiative has not been taken seriously by China. What they care more is how Taiwan responds to Japan's nationalization of the Diaoyutai and what actions are taken by Taipei.

The US position on the Senkaku/Diaoyutai islands has been ambiguous. The State Department often claims that the United States does not take a position on the question of the sovereignty and expect the claimants to resolve the dispute through peaceful means among themselves. However, American high officials frequently indicate that the Senkaku islands are subject to Article 5 of the US-Japan security treaty, which authorizes the US to help defend the areas that Japan administers. It is also interesting to see that Washington calls for the concerned parties having the responsibility to resolve disputes peacefully; lower tensions, but it shows no intention to play a mediating role.

With regard to Taiwan, Washington is aware that Taipei does not work with Beijing on the claim of sovereignty over the Diaoyutai islands even though the two sides of the Taiwan Strait hold the same position on the matter that the islands are the Chinese territory. Washington did not voice its concerns of Taiwan's fishermen protest activities; however after the event, it did not send senior officials to attend the annual bilateral defence conference held in the US. Some speculated that the absence of US officials was due to Taiwan's dispute with Japan over the islands and the irritation of water cannon battle between Taiwanese and Japanese coast guard vessel's. Taiwan's moves were perceived as deviating from American interests in East Asia.

Washington has not given any response to Ma's East China Sea Peace Initiative though some American scholars have shown interest and support. Many consider the proposal constructive and sensible and could be a useful way to deal with the dispute. But, on the other hand, they are not optimistic about the proposal being put into practice because of the limited role of Taiwan in regional politics. Anyway, it was a big surprise to Taipei seeing two US aircraft carrier battle groups deployed since mid-September in the Western Pacific, within easy reach of the Diaoyutai islands. What was the intention of Washington? It could have been a warning to China, a message to Taiwan, showing support to Japan or just a coincidence.

Conflict Resolution

Taiwan is aware of its weak position in the Asian regional relations, and does not play a major role in regional security. It also understands political sensitivities regarding territorial disputes. A solution to the conflict should be found through discussions. Failure to do so might pose a serious challenge to the Asia-Pacific regional peace and stability.

In my personal view, due to international politics it is hard to get official response and endorsement from the concerned parties for Ma's peace initiative. Nevertheless, if the peace initiative is considered helpful and if the concerned parties are willing to engage peacefully - bilaterally or trilaterally; officially or unofficially – Ma's proposal will do the job. The main point is to find a way to defuse the clash and pave way for peaceful talks.

Session III: Discussion

Panel-2

Issue Raised

Is US foreign policy creating space for China because US is aiming for regional powers to take over. In this scenario when states affected by Chinese territorial claims cannot come together how can they counter China?

Response

Yes, one can say to some extent that US regional policy is creating a vacuum for China to play its role but at the same time, China is also conscious about its foreign policy in the region where US interests are still dominant.

Issue Raised

Senkaku Islands are in news for the last few days due to dispute between China and Japan. The Islands have strategic importance. China can use these as havens for submarines.

Responses

(a) Japan and the US recognize the importance of Senkaku Islands. The Japanese are worried as to whether or not US support for issue would be forthcoming. However; theUS wants Japan to defend the Islands relying on their own security forces.

(b) The location of Senkaku Islands is important from military perspective, to control China's naval forces. And so it is important for Japan, South Korea and Taiwan to understand the importance of these islands.

Issue Raised

The US is engaging itself into activities all over the world. In view of her diversified presence globally; what factors are leading her to reduce presence in Asia-Pacific-Region?

Responses

(a) The US presence is not lessening globally. The US is more powerful than China. The US has the capacity to dominate the region provided it has the will to do so.

(b) The US focus is on smart power which is a combination of hard and soft powers. The US alone cannot ensure security without support of countries in the Asia-Pacific-Region.

Issue Raised

Will there be wars in the Asia-Pacific-Region? Can this turn into a nuclear war?

Response

The arms race is building up in the Asia-Pacific but it does not seem to be leading to a war. There may be some minor clashes but these will not lead to a nuclear war.

Issue Raised

Budget is not an important indicator as there can be technological asymmetry. Will increase in budget lead to insecurity in the region?

Responses

(a) Budget may not be the only indicator but given the time span which was chosen, budget as this, became an important factor. Technology is important and can play its role.

(b) The technological change is very essential as near parity in technology can bring symmetry in power among countries.

Session-III

Panel-2

Chairman's Concluding Remarks

Major General Dato' Pahlawan Dr. William R. Stevenson

The world is changing and the nature of emerging challenges is also changing. I hope that there will be no war and world will be a safer place to live in. I expect that there will be resolution of problems and issues through amicable discussions. I thank all the participants for their valuable comments.

Valedictory Address

Shri Asoke Mukerji, Special Secretary on behalf of Shri Ranjan Mathai, Foreign Secretary, Government of India

I am here to talk to you on behalf of Mr. Ranjan Mathai. I am very thankful to the USI and especially Lt Gen P K Singh for calling me to talk on the issue of **"Trade, Commerce and Security in the Asia-Pacific-Region"**. I complement USI for taking up such a multi-disciplinary theme. I am sure, you must have gained and enriched through discussions. At present, India is hosting foreign minister level meeting of the IOR-ARC countries in which 20 countries are participating. The conference is closely associated with the theme that this seminar has discussed. The Asia-Pacific-Region is becoming increasingly significant and hence we are hosting India- ASEAN summit in the month of December, 2012. India is part of EAS, which is driven by ASEAN. We strongly support the strategic dialogue among India and Asia-Pacific countries. We believe that there are five priority areas for engagement. Those are energy, finance, education, transportation, natural disasters and comprehensive economic partnerships.

It is very important for the region to have exchange of views among India and Asia-Pacific countries. Our Prime Minister Dr. Manmohan Singh has proposed the idea of Virtual Asian Economic community. We also think that Pan-Asian FTA should be the starting point of this community. There is also multi-fold increase in the energy demand for India. And from this perspective Indian engagement with Asia-Pacific-Region is very important.

The Asia Pacific region is experiencing major challenges, security of SLOCs is important for sustainable trade and commerce. Freedom of navigation is also of paramount concern. In this context, piracy at sea is of concern for India and for the region. We are in the process of replacing anti-piracy domestic legislation which has been in vogue since colonial times. There should be special focus on security of Choke-points like Malacca and Sundae straits.

Another challenge is interstate dispute for resources. South China Sea is cause of concern from this perspective. Rivalry between China and the US has already set alarm bells ringing. Non-traditional threats like terrorism, proliferation of WMD, drug trafficking, security of infrastructure like ports and cyber space security are some of the new areas that are vital for security. At the same time environmental degradation, issue of climate change need to be taken seriously. In case of climate change, India has made its position clear and follows the principle of common but differentiated responsibilities. We are working towards comprehensive regional security architecture in the Asia-Pacific-Region.

There are four vectors of India's engagement with Asia in the coming months. They are first, with the central Asia through the new silk route. The second is the Indian Ocean Rim, third is West Asia, where six million Indian passport holders are present and is of importance for India's energy needs. The fourth is the Asia-Pacific-Region. India has played a major role in the past; we are playing in the present and would be playing in the future.

Vote of Thanks

Lt Gen PK Singh, PVSM, AVSM (Retd), Director, USI

Good afternoon, Ladies and Gentleman, I thank my foreign participants who have taken the trouble to come to USI for this Seminar. I specially thank my friends from Vietnam and Malaysia for their presence. I take this opportunity to thank MEA for their continuous support to USI for organizing the events. We expect some outcome from these seminars where we can discuss and take forward these relations bilaterally and then multilaterally. The seminar brought issues related to trade, commerce and security within the Asia Pacific region. The discussion enlightened us to know about linkages between trade, commerce and security. During the seminar we came across large number of differences of opinions among panellists. But at the same time we were lucky enough to find some similarities of opinion among diverse countries.

There were many issues that were not touched upon during the seminar like, what if other countries go nuclear? What happens if Japan goes nuclear? Or South Korea goes nuclear. These issues were not discussed in this seminar. Hopefully they will be covered in next seminar. I finally thank all of you for attending this seminar and making it a grand success. I would thank specially Ashok Mukherjee for his valuable words.

Vote of Thanks

www.ingramcontent.com/pod-product-compliance
Lightning Source LLC
Chambersburg PA
CBHW020539270326
41927CB00006B/647